D1536270

Handing on the Faith in an Ecumenical World

Resources for Catholic Administrators and Religious Educators in Serving Christian Unity in School and Parish

Brother Jeffrey Gros, FSC

National Catholic Educational Association

Dedicated to the Memory of

Brother Theodore Drahmann FSC
(1921-2002)

And to All Catholic Administrators Who

Like Him Place Handing on the Faith

At the Center of Their Ministry

In the Church

Contents

Preface   vii

Chapter I   Introduction   1

Chapter II   Catholic Vision and Heritage   11
                Catholic Theological Basis for Ecumenical
                    Formation   16
                Resources   18

Chapter III   The Role of the Administrator   21
                Faith Community Formation   21
                Staff Selection and Development   23
                Policies and Programs   26
                Sacramental Policies   30

Chapter IV   The Religion Curriculum   37
                Cultural Differences   38
                Catechetical Renewal   38
                Elements of Ecumenical Catechesis   39
                Principles for Ecumenical Catechesis   41
                Eastern Churches   43
                Ethical Formation in an Ecumenical Context   44
                Catechetical Challenges   44

Chapter V   The Parish Directors of Religious Education   45
                Rite of Christian Initiation for Adults   47
                Non-Catholics Associated with Parish
                    Catechetical Programs   49
                Marriage Preparation   49
                Other Christian Ministers   51

Chapter VI   Fellow Christians in Catholic Schools   53
                Students   55
                Parents   59
                Faculty   61

Chapter VII   Concerns in Catholic Elementary Education   65

Chapter VIII   Concerns in Catholic Secondary Education   71

Chapter IX   Catholic Higher Education   75

Chapter X   Conclusion   79

                Notes   81

C atechesis is always to assume an "ecumenical dimension" everywhere, according to the *General Directory for Catechesis.* (GDC 1997) To help Catholic educators and catechetical leaders everywhere better understand what that means, the Department of Religious Education is pleased to present this book in a new series titled, For Religious Educators.

I thank Brother Jeffrey Gros, FSC, for his authorship of *Handing on the Faith in an Ecumenical World,* the first book in this series. He has succeeded in synthesizing important developments in the Church regarding ecumenism for front line educators. I am confident that this book will be an indispensable resource for teachers and catechists as they form others in faith, for local principals and parish catechetical leaders (DREs) as they provide ongoing faith formation opportunities for their teachers and catechists, and for diocesan chief administrators as they take a long view regarding how to better educate religious educators about the Church's ecumenical teachings.

I also want to thank Steve Palmer and Bernadette Laniak in the Department of Religious Education for editorial assistance and Mary Twillman for her expertise with the cover, design and production of the text.

Diana Dudoit Raiche
Executive Director
Department of Religious Education

Introduction

The National Catholic Educational Association serves the Church well by living out its mission of handing on the Catholic faith. By providing materials to support the mission of Catholic schools and parish religious educators and education programs, the NCEA strengthens and enriches the essential ministry of the Church in evangelization and catechesis.

Since the Second Vatican Council, the NCEA has assisted the schools and parishes in promoting renewal of the liturgy; Catholic social teaching; the enhanced role of the laity in boards, teaching and administration; the educational dimensions of ecumenical reconciliation; the school as faith community; and the massive renewal of catechetics. This short volume is another contribution to enabling schools and parishes to carry forward the ecumenical component of their educational task, one richly supported by the Magisterium of the Church.

This book is a resource for educators in knowing the position of the Catholic Church on ecumenical formation and the resources suggested for the educational task. Both ecumenical commitments – the Catholic Church's commitment to visible unity with fellow Christians, and interfaith outreach – the Catholic Church's mission to dialogue and collaborate with non-Christian believers, are important elements, integral to Catholic evangelization. With the society in which we live, internationally and locally, becoming increasingly pluralistic, both ecumenical commitment to unity with fellow Christians and learning to live peacefully, in mutual understanding with peoples of other faiths, Catholic education equips our people for both of these dimensions of Catholic life. However, this volume will deal only with Christian unity, ecumenism properly so-called. We will use the term "fellow Christians," as the Holy Father does, or "Christians of other churches," in preference to "non-Catholic" or even "separated brethren," the designation of the Second Vatican Council. We may not be in full communion or share in the fullness of the faith, sacraments and church order of these fellow Christians, but we recognize the real communion in Christ that binds us together.

Graduates of Catholic schools and religious education programs now will live in a Christian world with members of other churches. They will work together, engage in common projects in the community, attend one another's churches for weddings and funerals, marry one another, and pray for the unity of their churches. Religious formation prepares young people to live out of a deep sense of their Catholic faith in a world where the Church lives among other Christians and is committed to deeper relations with them.

This book is designed for religious educators, Catholic administrators, campus ministers and parish directors of religious education. It also provides a resource that might be of use to Catholic school subject area teachers, volunteer catechists, parents and board members in support of this dimension of their ministry in Catholic education.

When I began teaching in 1959, the Second Vatican Council had only been announced; the expectations were unclear, and the Catholic schools were at their peak. While I was growing up in Memphis, Tennessee, all Catholic students were required to be in a Catholic school. Parents, like mine, would see that the Catholic education of their children was assured before moving from an apartment into a house. We lived out this Catholic faith in a community that was 95 % Protestant. When I began teaching in the Archdiocese of Chicago, I entered into my first Catholic school where all the faculty and students were Catholic.

In Memphis every Catholic grade school and high school had significant numbers of Protestant teachers and students, and in high school there were even a good number of Jewish students. The Catholic environment was much more welcoming for these Jewish students than the evangelical Protestant-dominated public schools. There was never any doubt about our Catholic identity, as a minority in this largely fundamentalist environment.

The fact that the student body and faculty were pluralistic made our Catholic identity even stronger. Likewise, it gave a strong witness to the wider community both of the strength and security of our Catholic faith, as different as it might be, and the openness of the Catholic Church to share its mission with fellow Christians and others of good will.

With friends in the Protestant and Jewish community, my formation in Minnesota where the liturgical movement was well developed, and beginning teaching in Chicago where the catechetical movement was well founded long before the Council, there was a great deal of enthusiasm about ecumenical, interreligious, liturgical and catechetical reform in 1959.

As a young Catholic school teacher, I was to learn that this enthusiasm was not universal. The formation of all Catholic teachers was not such that catechetical, biblical, liturgical, ecumenical and social renewal came easily. Indeed, many of us in the theological disciplines – the first generation of laity and lay religious to be so trained – spent decades in renewal programs for teachers, clergy, parents and religious, preparing them to pass on the faith in changing times.

This period was a particular burden for Catholic school administrators and for the parish directors of religious education. As Catholic catechesis shifted from: the responsibility of religious to lay professional ecclesial ministers; from the school room to parish religious education; and from the contained Catholic, ethnic, neighborhood parishes to suburban pluralistic communities; so challenges to Catholic identity, the focus of educator-formation and clarity of mission also emerged.

During the decades after the Council, new reforms were being presented seemingly almost daily. Each new sacramental reform, each new occasion for social witness, each new structure for lay participation and each new ecumenical agreement, made demands on those charged with handing on the faith and administration of Catholic institutions.

Deepened relations with other churches, greater roles for the laity, more participation in the liturgy, a higher profile for the Church in witness to the Gospel calling to justice and peace and a deeper Christ centered catechesis, were openings to a richer vision of Catholicism for many. For the busy administrator, the harried high school or elementary religion teacher, or the – often newly minted – parish director of religious education, the challenge often seemed overwhelming. The developments in Catholic leadership and changes in perspectives also complicated educational developments.

The last decade of the twentieth century has seen the challenge of the implementation of the *Catechism of the Catholic Church*, an attempt to forge a new partnership between the U.S. bishops and the text book publishers, and readjustment of priorities in the liturgical renewal. These developments, along with the publication of *Directory for the Application of Principles and Norms on Ecumenism* and the maturity of various ecumenical dialogues, all provide for positive possibilities. They also can be seen as challenges. The Catholic educational world is stretched in our ability to adapt and provide resources for the Catholic catechist and classroom teacher. It is hoped that this short overview will be a practical and helpful contribution in this calling.

"Christ the Lord founded one Church and one Church only." (Decree on Ecumenism 1) Thus, it is God's will that the Christian churches be united. Our one baptism into Christ is the foundation for communion among Christians. At the Holy Spirit's prompting, the Catholic Church and many Christian communities are striving to achieve that unity which is Christ's gift to the Church. This is the blessing and the challenge of the ecumenical movement.

The Catholic Church is committed to the long pilgrimage to full reconciliation among all Christian churches through the process of collaboration, prayer and dialogue. This is particularly important where Catholics are a majority in the community. The Catholic school is a privileged place for spiritual formation, dialogue and education. The parish is the place where the Christian community lives out its life, and where relations with other communities are initiated and nurtured.

The word ecumenical comes from the Greek word (*ecumene*) meaning the whole inhabited earth. It began to be used by the Christians in the early Church to designate universal, or the whole Christian community worldwide, thus *ecumenical* councils. Since the last century it has been used to designate the call for the universal unity of the Christian Church, especially overcoming the divisions of East and West and of the Reformation of the sixteenth century.

It is important to distinguish, for catechists and for students, between *interfaith* and *ecumenical*. The former designates mutual understanding and collaboration with the world's religions outside of Christianity. *Ecumenical* means the collaboration of Christians in prayer and witness and their search for full reconciliation of our churches in Christ.

The theology of the Church articulated by the Catholic Church and now current in ecumenical conversations is that of communion (*koinonia*). It is grounded in the communion of Father, Son and Holy Spirit, and the communion between the baptized and the Trinity in Christ's saving death and resurrection.

Catholics believe in the real, but imperfect, communion among all baptized Christians, and the call of all Christian churches to full communion in common faith, sacramental life and witness. Everyone catechized in the Catholic faith will need to experience conversion toward this zeal for unity as central to Catholic identity, and the goal of full communion as the horizon of their hopes for the Church.[1]

Today, loyalty to the Catholic vision of education in our parishes and schools entails the commitment to the goal of visible unity among Christians, the nurturing of a firm faith in the Church and its commitment to dialogue, and zeal to know and seek unity with all other followers of Jesus Christ.

Pope John Paul II emphasizes this commitment as central to the Catholic identity which is fostered in the Catholic schools and religious education programs:

> ...it is absolutely clear that ecumenism, the movement promoting Christian Unity, is not just some sort of "appendix" which is added to the Church's traditional activity. Rather, ecumenism is an organic part of her life and work and, consequently, must pervade all that she is and does; it must be like the fruit borne by a healthy and flourishing tree which grows to its full stature.

> The quest for Christian unity is not a matter of choice or expediency, but a duty which springs from the very nature of the Christian community.

> Concern for restoring unity pertains to the whole church, faithful and clergy alike. It extends to everyone, according to the ability of each, whether it be exercised in daily Christian living or in theological and historical studies.[2]

There has been a rather thorough development in Catholic commitments from the time of the Council, through the initiatives of the Holy See in providing directives, including incentives for the schools and religious communities, through the official dialogues with other Christian communities; and through the promotion of an ecumenical dimension to the spirituality of all Catholics.

The 1993 *Directory for the Application of Principles and Norms on Ecumenism* provides helpful clarity:

> The school, of every kind and grade, should give an ecumenical dimension to its religious teaching, and should aim in its own way to train hearts and minds in human and religious values, educating for dialogue, for peace and for personal relationships.

> a) The spirit of charity, of respect and of dialogue demands the elimination of language and prejudices which distort the image of other Christians. This holds especially for Catholic schools where the young

must grow in faith, in prayer and in resolve to put into practice the Christian Gospel of unity. They should be taught genuine ecumenism, according to the doctrine of the Catholic Church.

b) Where possible, in collaboration with other teachers, different subjects, e.g. history and art, should be treated in a way that underlines the ecumenical problems in a spirit of dialogue and unity. To this end it is also desirable that teachers be correctly and adequately informed about the origins, history and doctrines of other Churches and ecclesial Communities especially those that exist in their region.[3]

In this short volume we will indicate some of the principles that may help the Catholic schools and parish educational programs nurture the goal of visible unity as central to Catholic identity. Issues of administrative leadership, sacramental sharing, fellow Christians who are not Catholic, curriculum and higher education will be broached.

The goal of the Catholic Church in the ecumenical movement is full communion with all Christians:

The Catholic Church solemnly pledged itself to work for Christian unity at the Second Vatican Council. The Decree *Unitatis Redintegratio* explains how the unity that Christ wishes for his Church is brought about "through the faithful preaching of the Gospel by the Apostles and their successors—the Bishops with Peter's successor at their head—through their administering the sacraments, and through their governing in love", and defines this unity as consisting of the "confession of one faith,... the common celebration of divine worship,... the fraternal harmony of the family of God." This unity which of its very nature requires full visible communion of all Christians is the ultimate goal of the ecumenical movement. The Council affirms that this unity by no means requires the sacrifice of the rich diversity of spirituality, discipline, liturgical rites and elaborations of revealed truth that has grown up among Christians in the measure that this diversity remains faithful to the apostolic Tradition.[4]

That is, Catholics recognize a spiritual unity among all Christians, but also see God's will for a visible, sacramental unity in this world as well. Our approach to this visible unity is dialogue. Christians have been united in different ways, over the two thousand years of history, so we do not expect a

united Church to look just like the Catholic Church looks today
(or for that matter, at any other time in its history), but we do
expect there to be full agreement on: 1) the Apostolic Faith; 2)
the sacraments; and 3) the decision-making role of the bishops
in communion with the Holy Father. Our emphasis as Catholics
is on dialogue with other churches to resolve the issues that
have traditionally divided us. While some individuals will move
from one church to another out of conscientious conviction, we
respect the convictions of others and the churches that nourish
their faith and bring them salvation in Jesus Christ.

In the United States, churches experience a certain religious
illiteracy among our people. With fewer Catholics in our schools,
and many not even participating in the parish religious education
program, we are challenged to provide a core of committed
Catholics who are deeply evangelized in their commitment to the
Gospel and catechized in the content of the Church's teaching.

In American society this is a common ecumenical challenge
which we share with other Christian churches. Our Catholic
people need to know both our common faith with other
Christians and the areas where issues need to be resolved.
Christians can hardly resolve our differences if our people do
not know the core of the faith and do not even realize what has
divided us in the past. How do Christians collaborate to address
the problem of the void of religious knowledge among Christians
in our society?

Sociologists have documented this challenge to Catholic
identity in a way that lays a challenge before us as educators:

> The criteria surrounding Catholic identity – what is
> "core" and obligatory to the faith, what is and what is not
> legitimate in belief and practice, who does and who does
> not belong – have become more problematic in the last
> four decades. Catholic identity, once confined to clearly
> defined categories, is now as loosely marked as that of
> other mainline religious traditions.[5]

Two conflicting temptations beset the Catholic educator:
1) a sectarian tendency; and 2) a denominational indifferentism.

> 1) A tendency is prevalent in the polarized and politicized
> religious atmosphere in many of the churches, including
> Catholic, to sacrifice authentic Catholic identity to a
> sectarian stance that defines Catholicism over against
> other Christians. As Peter Phan notes: Given the
> recent remarkable progress in ecumenical dialogue,
> doctrines and structures that at one time were regarded
> as exclusive properties of the Catholic Church are
> today becoming common possessions of many in the

mainline Christian churches. Rather than differentiation and exclusiveness, I conceive Catholic identity as intensification and deepening... [Dialogues] do not constitute a threat to Catholic identity; rather they provide a necessary means and the opportunities for deepening and intensifying the Catholic identity, not over or against others, but with them.[6]

In some situations, where other churches predominate, there can be a retreat from the ecumenical ideals of the Catholic Church because we are a beleaguered minority in an oppressive situation. In still other cultural contexts, outreach to other Christians is seen as irrelevant, or even a distraction, because the vast majority of people are Catholics, at least in a cultural sense. In all of these situations, Catholic educators are challenged both to adapt to the culture and to empower their students with an appropriate sense of their own faith, and a zeal for unity with other Christians.

Christian identity and affiliation with a specific tradition is a challenge for all Christians. There is a sectarian option that would make one's own community the center of the Christian universe, rather than Christ and the faith of the Church through the ages. Catholics are particularly tempted to sectarianism and triumphalism because of our theological claims and because of our large size, worldwide extension and isolation in some countries and neighborhoods where we are the majority.

However, we also encounter an anti-ecumenical attitude in some Evangelicals who do not want to dialogue and will even proselytize Catholics. As the largest Church in the world and in the United States, Catholics have a particular responsibility. Our size and our claims press us to be more ecumenical and respectful, while opening ourselves to dialogue and renewal. For catechesis, this means keeping both a clear identity and an open spirit as the goal of our formation.

It is particularly important in communities that are majority Catholic, or among new immigrants coming from places where Catholics may be the majority, like Latin America or Eastern Europe, to help students to see relationships with fellow Christians as an integral value in Catholic life. There are important differences among ecumenical fellow Christians who share the goal of full communion; those fellow Christians who are not ecumenical and even sometimes anti-Catholic; and non-Christian groups, like Witnesses and Mormons. In parts of the world where Catholics predominate, these differences are not always clear in Catholic catechesis and preaching.

2) The other option that plagues Christian cultures is what we have classically called "indifference." In some secularized and pluralistic places in the United States, Catholicism often is understood as just another denomination, where we live and let live. Some might say: "The different churches are just one expression of the Church, which is a spiritual unity where full communion is only realized in heaven." From this perspective there is an indifference to the unity of the Church and complacency with Christian divisions. People see one church is as good as another, with no reason to embark on the arduous pilgrimage toward that unity for which Christ so fervently prayed. "Fewer young adult Catholics believe that it is important to be Catholic."[7] The Catholic educator will help students and faculty understand the importance of the Catholic faith, the Christian context of a local situation, and to reach out in dialogue and mutual respect where this is possible.

When we say "The Catholic Church believes…" we are not saying that we affirm one among many Christian options. Rather we are affirming that we believe that this is the "faith of the church through the ages," the faith that is truly universal (catholic). Thus, It Is the faith we share with Protestants and Orthodox about the Scripture, the Trinity and divinity of Christ, etc. Other churches may affirm interpretations of the "catholic faith," which are different from ours, and therefore we must enter into dialogue. We believe these things because they are true, not because they somehow belong to our Church, or because they necessarily differ from the faith of other Christians. On the other hand, what we believe is not just one, subjective, affirmation among many options.

Catholicism has a clearly different tradition from evangelical Protestantism, with its individualistic, personal conversion orientation, and some forms of classical Protestantism, where the divisions of history are relativized in the face of God's call for peace among Christians. Ecumenism does not mean mere tolerance, any more than it means sectarian isolation.

Neither sectarianism nor indifferentism is the Catholic way. The current institutional suspicion, that is so rife in some cultures, can make it difficult to engender a real sense of Catholic and ecumenical community. "As the boundaries of Catholicism become weaker and more diffuse, preserving and transmitting the tradition's norms become more difficult."[8]

True ecumenical respect entails sensitivity to one's own identity, history, diversity and openness to the future.

In the United States the pluralistic context and a sense of individual initiative characterizing the culture have developed an environment where a host of independent churches of a variety of types exists. They range from the store front preacher of the urban neighborhood to the suburban megachurches. This Christian diversity requires considerable ecumenical discernment for Catholic educators. This is especially true in working with immigrant communities.

The Catholic Church is the largest religious body in the U.S. Some Catholics still think as a minority since there are more people here who are not Catholic, unlike Latin America or southern Europe. There is no Christian body that sees itself as a majority next to the enormous number of Catholics.

This places a certain ecumenical leadership in Catholic hands, and a need for sensitivity about Catholic numbers and power, which are greater than any other religious community in the U.S.

Catholic Vision and Heritage

After more than thirty years on the pilgrimage toward Christian unity, there is much to be learned and much to be taught. Certainly the developments of Christian relationships to one another and the Catholic Church's ecumenical pilgrimage are testimony to God's marvelous providence.

Catholic education through the Catholic school and parish religion program is an important locus for nurturing the conversion that is necessary for the ecumenical vision among Christians, Catholic or not. Each is also the place for catechetical instruction that gives this vision the religious, spiritual and experiential content of the ecumenical movement. The Catholic school and parish religious education program touches hearts, but it also informs minds about the hopes and progress of the churches together in response to Christ's prayer.

The Council itself placed conversion at the center of the ecumenical enterprise:

¶ 7. There can be no ecumenism worthy of the name without a change of heart. For it is from renewal of the inner life of our minds, from self-denial and an unstinted love that desires of unity take their rise and develop in a mature way. We should therefore pray to the Holy Spirit for the grace to be genuinely self-denying, humble, gentle in the service of others, and to have an attitude of brotherly generosity towards them. St. Paul says: "I, therefore, a prisoner for the Lord, beg you to lead a life worthy of the calling to which you have been called, with all humility and meekness, with patience, forbearing one another in love, eager to maintain the unity of the spirit in the bond of peace." (Eph. 4, 1-3)…

The words of St. John hold good about sins against unity: "If we say we have not sinned, we make him a liar, and his word is not in us."(1 Jn. 1, 10) So we humbly beg pardon of God and of our separated brethren, just as we forgive them that trespass against us.

All the faithful should remember that the more effort they make to live holier lives according to the Gospel, the better will they further Christian unity and put it into practice. For the closer their union with the Father, the Word and the Spirit, the more deeply and easily will they be able to grow in mutual brotherly love.

¶ 8. This change of heart and holiness of life, along with public and private prayer for the unity of Christians, should be regarded as the soul of the whole ecumenical movement, and merits the name, "spiritual ecumenism." [9]

Conversion to Christ entails faith in the Church and participation in its mission:

¶ 55. Faith involves a change of life, a *metanoia*, that is a profound transformation of mind and heart; it causes the believer to live that conversion. This transformation of life manifests itself at all levels of the Christian's existence: in his interior life of adoration and acceptance of the divine will, in his action, participation in the mission of the Church, in his married and family life; in his professional life; in fulfilling economic and social responsibilities. [10]

For Catholics, often in contrast to some of our evangelical fellow Christians, work for the unity of Christians is integral to evangelization as we understand it: "The new evangelization is the order of the day ...The task of evangelization involves moving toward each other and moving together as Christians, and it must begin from within; evangelization and unity, evangelization and ecumenism are indissolubly linked with each other....Because the question of the new evangelization is very close to my heart, as bishop of Rome, I consider overcoming the divisions of Christianity 'one of the pastoral priorities.'" (Pope John Paul II, Germany, July, 1996) Christians work together to catechize their own people, help them understand the Gospel call to unity and prepare them for sharing the Gospel with alienated Christians and nonbelievers.

The Catholic Church has formal dialogues with churches of both East and West. Among the Eastern churches are the Assyrian, Eastern and Oriental Orthodox churches. There are also dialogues with the Polish National Catholic Church; Anglicans (Episcopalians), Lutherans, Methodists, Reformed, Presbyterian, United Church of Christ, Disciples of Christ, Southern Baptists and Pentecostals. The Church relates to a wide range of other churches through the Faith and Order Commissions of the World and National Councils of Churches to which the Catholic Church has belonged since 1968.

The *General Directory for Catechesis* (1997) summarizes the principles that guide Catholic schools and religious education programs. These principles are spelled out in more detail in the documents summarized in the resources section:

¶ 197. Every Christian community, by the mere fact of being what it is, is moved by the Spirit to recognize its ecumenical vocation in the circumstances in which it finds itself, by participating in ecumenical dialogue and initiatives to foster the unity of Christians. Catechesis, therefore, is always called to assume an "ecumenical dimension" everywhere. This is done, firstly, by an exposition of all of Revelation, of which the Catholic Church conserves the deposit, while respecting the hierarchy of truths. In the second place, catechesis brings to the fore that unity of faith which exists between Christians and explains the divisions existing between them and the steps being taken to overcome them. Catechesis also arouses and nourishes a true desire for unity, particularly with the love of Sacred Scripture. Finally, it prepares children, young people and adults to live in contact with brothers and sisters of other confessions, by having them cultivate both their own Catholic identity and respect for the faith of others.[11]

For some of our Catholic schools church unity is not seen, existentially, as a pressing need because the vast majority of students are Catholic. By definition, parish religious education programs are primarily Catholic. However, in Catholic environments where there are no Christians from other churches, ecumenism is particularly important because students will grow up and live in a pluralistic world. Catholics are committed to the unity of Christians by their very commitment to Christ and to the mission of the Church as articulated in the Council. A school or religious education program should be an environment that encourages conversion of heart to Christ, to the Church's mission and to the ecumenical dimension of that mission.

On the other hand, where there are fellow Christians in our schools, and where non-Catholic parents participate in the religious education programming of the parish, there is a particular advantage for the educational mission of the Church, as the late Sister Thea Bowman says so eloquently:

> The presence of persons (students, parents, teachers) from the variety of religious and cultural traditions within the close community of the Catholic school [and one might add religious education program] can provide for all our children from their earliest years a supportive environment in which to grow in mutual understanding as well as the opportunity for true ecumenical dialogue and collaboration on an on-going basis. The presence of persons from the variety of traditions can challenge us:

> - To be who we say we are as Christian – loving, open, respectful of persons, concerned about the total human community;
> - To share the light of faith in the mutuality of evangelization;
> - To clarify our own convictions and commitments as Catholics;
> - To develop attitudes, appreciations and skills requisite to ecumenical and cross-cultural communication and cooperation.[12]

The catechetical work also is deeply contextual, providing sensitivity to the concrete community reality in which the parish and school live, according to the *General Directory:*

> In developing this community sense, catechesis takes special note of the ecumenical dimension and encourages fraternal attitudes toward members of other Christian churches and ecclesial communities. Thus catechesis in pursuing this objective should give a clear exposition of all the Church's doctrine and avoid formulations or expressions that might give rise to error. It also implies "a suitable knowledge of other confessions," with which there are shared elements of faith: "the written word of God, the life of grace, faith, hope and charity, and the other interior gifts of the Holy Spirit." Catechesis will possess an ecumenical dimension in the measure in which it arouses and

nourishes "a true desire for unity," not easy irenicism, but perfect unity, when the Lord himself wills it and by those means by which he wishes that it should be brought about.[13]

The *General Directory* also speaks of adult catechesis and the centrality of the *Rite of Christian Initiation for Adults*. It emphasizes the appropriate distinctions and care that needs to be taken of both the ecumenical dimension of adult catechesis, and the sensitivity to Christians coming into full communion in the RCIA, who are not catechumens properly so-called. (# 133) For example, it is suggested that those coming into full communion be initiated at a different time and in a different ritual than those being baptized. In the rites, it would be inappropriate to present the creed or the bible to a Christian who has already been nurtured in the Christian faith and scriptures, even if in another church than the Catholic Church.

Catholic education, of course, is a doctrinal matter as well as one of the heart. There is a content to the heritage we pass on, as emphasized by the *Catechism* and the *General Directory* (# 119 ff.). For this reason the 1993 *Directory for the Application of Principles and Norms on Ecumenism* has a whole chapter on the theological commitments of the Catholic Church, as well as one on ecumenical formation.

Not only has the Catholic Church clarified its own self understanding as a communion (*koinonia*), including its relationship with other churches and ecclesial communities, it has also sponsored theological dialogues since 1965 which have opened up clear doctrinal agreements and overcome some historical problems. These dialogues are important contributions to our understanding of the faith and our communication of this understanding to new generations.

Specific relationships with ecumenical partners have developed on parish, diocesan, national levels, and at the level of the universal church. All of these are resources for handing on this heritage and provide experiences for those learning their faith to deepen their understanding and commitment.

It is the task of the bishops' conferences and the Holy See to carry on these dialogues and build these relationships. However, every diocese and parish has the challenge to build local relationships and to study the results of these dialogues. It is the challenge of the Catholic educator and her or his colleagues in other churches to make these theological agreements and relationships come alive in the experience, hopes and understanding of our Christian people.

Catholic Theological Basis for Ecumenical Formation

The quest for Christian unity is not a program of study, though it does have its catechetical component. It is not merely an institutional matter, though it has implications for all of our Catholic institutional life. It is above all an attitude of mind a conversion of heart.

The Holy Father continually reminds Catholics that we are committed irrevocably to the full, visible unity of the Christian churches, that ecumenism is integral to Catholic identity. The Magisterium has been very strong in its support of Catholic ecumenism and the dialogues that have developed since the Council.

The ecumenical dimension of the faith life of our educational ministries is not left in the hands of catechists, chaplains and campus ministers alone. If we do not have a full faculty and staff at the Catholic school with a basic commitment and support of Catholic values and the commitment of the Church, in this case to the unity of Christians, then we are undermining our mission from within.

In building the Catholic faith community in the school, for example, we strive to foster a sacramental consciousness. This entails learning to live out the real, but imperfect, communion Catholics share with all baptized Christians. The experience of communion is learned through direct personal experience, common prayer with other Christians, and appreciation of their leaders. How these experiences of ecumenism are made an integral part of the administrative plan of a particular ministry is a very practical decision adapted to the culture, needs and challenges of each situation.

The ecumenical dimension of the Catholic education's mission is situated squarely in the center of the teaching of the Catholic Church about education, as summarized by Monsignor James Hawker in an earlier NCEA contribution to assisting the schools in dealing with other Christians in the school:

- The Catholic school is identified with the Church as a structured community.
- The Catholic school participates uniquely in the pastoral/educational mission of the Church.
- The Catholic school is a developing community of Faith, founded upon Jesus Christ – His person and message, His vision and values.
- The Catholic school is an evangelizing community within which the spirit of the Gospel is shared and experienced, taught and caught.

- The Catholic school is a catechizing community within which the basic teachings of Christ and His Church are shared.
- The Catholic school is a grace-filled setting within which there is a synthesis of culture and faith and a synthesis of faith and life.
- The Catholic school is staffed by committed Catholics, whether lay, religious or priests.
- The Catholic school is staffed, in some instances, by non-Catholics who accept and strive to fulfill the goals of Catholic education and who participate in the prayer life of the community to the extent they are able.[14]

An element of this grace-filled setting is an enthusiasm for unity among Christians. The Catholic passion for unity is one of the elements that characterizes the shifts in the understanding of the Church emerging from the Council, like the renewal of the liturgy, empowering of the lay faithful, and understanding the quest for peace and justice, as integral to evangelization.

- We recognize the real but imperfect communion that exists between the Catholic Church and other churches and ecclesial communities, and we have begun to live into a deeper communion.
- We no longer speak of "separated brethren" but of "fellow Christians."
- Common Baptism, those things we share in faith and our common scripture help Catholic identity to be formed within an understanding of our common Christianity.
- We have moved from an ecumenism of "return" to a mutual respect, using dialogue as the means for disclosing our agreements, and those things needing resolution on the pilgrimage toward that unity for which Christ prayed.
- Our theological understanding has shifted from seeing the Roman Catholic Church as the one, true Church to an affirmation of the fact that the one, true Church "subsists in" the Catholic Church, but that elements of the true Church are alive and saving in other churches, and that we are all wounded while the scandal of division remains.
- We celebrate the progress that has been made with Protestant, Orthodox and Anglican fellow pilgrims toward full communion.
- Catholics avoid proselytism or any triumphalism that sets one Christian community against another.

Resources

In the years since the Council and its Decrees on Education and on Ecumenism, specific directives have continued to emerge to strengthen and clarify the Church's mission in serving the unity of the Church. During the 1990s there have been three very important documents: the 1993 *Directory for the Application of Principles and Norms on Ecumenism*, the 1995 encyclical *Ut Unum Sint*, and the 1998 *Ecumenical Dimension of Formation for Pastoral Workers*.[15] These reinforce the impetus for ecumenical education articulated in the *Ex Corde Ecclesiae* (1990), the *Catechism of the Catholic Church* (1992) and the *General Directory for Catechesis* (1997).

The ecumenical *Directory* brings together the policies articulated in a dozen different Vatican documents and introduces an important new chapter on ecumenical formation. The ecumenical *Directory* characterizes the ecumenical mission of the Church:

> The ecumenical movement is a grace of God, given by the Father in answer to the prayer of Jesus and supplication of the Church inspired by the Holy Spirit. While it is carried out within the general mission of the Church to unite humanity in Christ, its own specific field is the restoration of unity among Christians. Those who are baptized in the name of Christ are, by that very fact, called to commit themselves to the search for unity. Baptismal communion tends toward full ecclesial communion. To live our Baptism is to be caught up in Christ's mission of making all things one.[16]

The *Directory* is designed to "motivate, enlighten and guide this [ecumenical] activity," as well as to provide directives. It has been developed "in the light of the experience of the Church in the years since the Council and taking account of the present ecumenical situation." Diocesan ecumenical commissions, ecumenical commissions within religious communities and special delegates with responsibility for promoting Christian unity in their sphere of action, are all suggested by the *Directory*.

After the ecumenical *Directory* was promulgated in 1993, a number of religious communities set up a commission and designated a liaison to promote the ecumenical work within their communities. The Jesuits have had such a position since the Council. These commissions and liaisons can be of particular help in schools and parishes sponsored by the specific religious community.

The school and parish religious education program will find a resource in collaboration with diocesan ecumenical

programs, which as the *Directory* notes vary widely:
"The situations being dealt with in ecumenism are often
unprecedented, and vary from place to place and time to
time. The initiatives of the faithful in the ecumenical domain
are to be encouraged. But there is need for constant and
careful discernment by those who have ultimate responsibility
for the doctrine and the discipline of the Church."[17] We are in
the early decades of the reforms of Vatican II, so that we are
being surprised by the Holy Spirit by new developments each
day. We are also uncovering new challenges with which we
are called to deal in God's providence.

Pope John Paul devoted his twelfth encyclical letter in
1995 to Catholics worldwide on the unity of the Church, *Ut
Unum Sint*, in order to help us as Catholics and educators to
live up to our ecumenical vocation. This letter is a summary
of thirty years of Catholic participation in the ecumenical
movement. It recounts the irreversible commitments made
and the relationships developed. It outlines an agenda for
dialogue, while affirming that Christians share more than what
divides us. It encourages Catholics to see every Christian,
according to their position and formation, as called to serve
the unity of the Church. The ecumenical mission of the
Church is not to be an "appendix," but central to the life of the
Church.

Catholics no longer speak of "separated brethren" but
of fellow Christians. As will be noted below, the Holy Father
challenges us as educators especially, to help the Church
to "receive" the results of forty years of dialogue so that all
of our people can participate in the fruits of the Spirit that
have enriched all of our churches by our common witness,
dialogue and deepening spiritual ties with one another.[18]

Most recently, in this context of educational renewal for
Catholics, the Pontifical Council for Promoting Christian
Unity, the office in the Holy See responsible for ecumenism,
has developed a document, *The Ecumenical Dimension in
the Formation of Pastoral Workers*. It suggests that teachers
and all pastoral workers begin their studies with a course
on ecumenism, so that all Catholic theology and pastoral
practice is seen through the prism of a zeal for the unity of
the Church and an understanding of the Catholic faith in the
context of this ecumenical commitment. Implementing this
program provides a major challenge for our schools and
catechist training programs, for our in-service programs,
and for our collaboration with ecumenical partners. Catholic
formation programs will find in it principles and detailed
resources for filling out their training for leadership, faith

and mission. More will be said about its principles in the discussion of the catechetical curriculum. (Chapter IV)

Many schools and parishes use the annual Week of Prayer for Christian Unity as an opportunity to bring together Orthodox, Protestant and Anglican leaders for common prayer and possibly even some dialogue events. Many episcopal conferences collaborate with ecumenical groups in adapting the materials to their particular contexts.[19] Administrators can work with the diocesan ecumenical officer (each diocese as directed to appoint one) in seeing that the materials get out to each class, possibly with suggestions and resources. Schools and parishes can use the week of prayer as an "ecumenism awareness week," where other churches and our Catholic relationship with them can be explored.[20]

The *Catechism of the Catholic Church*, 1992 [CCC], a now familiar source provides a compendium from which much catechetical preparation and resources are drawn. It reiterates the Conciliar vision on ecumenism (815-855). It also articulates the doctrine on which our agreement with other Christians is based and our differences clarified.

It is to be interpreted and implemented in the light of the subsequent magisterial contributions noted above. Likewise, if the results of the ecumenical dialogues are "to become a common heritage," (UUS 80) as Pope John Paul II suggests, Catholic educators will need to provide resources for teaching and programs for catechists that relate these agreements among the Christian churches to the doctrinal elements of catechesis. (GDC 119 ff)

S tudents pick up their attitudes about other Christians and about zeal for Christian unity from the interests, openness and enthusiasm of the administrators and teachers as much as they learn in religion classes. The encouragement given by administrators, and the symbolic leadership provided by presidents and principals, is a factor in the ecumenical horizon developed in the faculty community. Modeling ecumenical openness, prayer for the unity of the Church and promotion of dialogue on the part of leadership, provides both students and faculty with role models for bringing these Catholic commitments into the daily life of the school and community.

Essential to Catholic faith community formation is creating a context for ecumenical conversion. As the Holy Father notes: "The entire life of Christians is marked by a concern for ecumenism; and they are called to let themselves be shaped, as it were, by that concern. ...there is a clear connection between renewal, conversion and reform...No Christian community can exempt itself from this call."[21]

Faith Community Formation

For the school and parish this means providing an environment where the commitment to the Catholic goal of visible unity, the Catholic openness to a dialogue of love and hospitality, and an enthusiasm about every step closer to the goal of unity among the churches, is an essential part of the atmosphere. The Catholic ecumenical climate is the unique responsibility of the administrative team, its leader and its entire faculty or team of catechists.

School and parish ecumenical services, during the Week of Prayer and at other times, ecumenical components to retreats, symbols of ecumenical events and developments in the religious decor of the school and parish, all contribute to the community's sense of the ecumenical component of Catholic communal identity.

The spirit of charity, of respect and of dialogue demands the elimination of language and prejudices which distort the image of other Christians. This holds especially for Catholic schools and religion programs where the young must grow in faith, in prayer and in resolve to put into practice the Christian Gospel of unity. They should be taught genuine ecumenism, according to the doctrine of the Catholic Church.

The relationships with other churches are constantly changing, mostly for the better. Therefore, attention to these relationships is an ongoing challenge. Even when there are setbacks in particular relationships, these are occasions for prayer for one another, and for deeper understanding among Christians.

As the ecumenical *Directory* notes: "Where ecumenical work is not being done, or not being done effectively, Catholics will seek to promote it. Where it is being opposed or hampered by sectarian attitudes and activities that lead to even greater divisions among those who confess the name of Christ, they should be patient and persevering."[22] From time to time, faculty and catechist meetings and staff retreats will provide a forum for updating, or signaling developments that are taking place, even when it may not be possible to provide any depth of engagement.

A faculty, catechist and staff community of faith is a necessary context in which all students experience the meaning of community:

> Students who attend the Catholic school should be assisted to understand the nature and to experience the meaning of Christian community. Each student should be respected as a unique and gifted creation of God. Students should be challenged to view and treat one another as brothers and sisters in the Lord. They should be helped to appreciate that the development of Christian community is a common responsibility shared by all who participate in the Catholic school.[23]

Not many will be able to follow the ecumenical developments of the Church in detail, nor are all equally responsible for the religious vision of the school or parish. However, the whole staff community needs to be attentive to this priority of the Church, and not leave it to specialized staff.

Creating a climate in the school and parish where other church leaders are common and welcome, provides an atmosphere that is both symbolic and carries an educational potential in itself. It is an advantage when the

Catholic school has other committed Christians among its faculty. Their witness to fellow colleagues through leading prayer and to students in ecumenical prayer services, can model the ecumenical community into which students are being initiated. Parish catechetical programs can take the advantage of children in interchurch families to connect with the congregations of one of the parents, or provide hospitality for ministers or priests known to students.

In a school that is all or predominantly Catholic, special effort will be necessary so that there are occasions for ministers and priests of other churches to participate in ecumenical services. In parishes where the neighborhood is largely Catholic, invitation to catechetical classes, or planning of common liturgical events will need to be developed intentionally. Opportunities for dialogue and occasions to visit other churches will need particular attention. The curriculum will have to be attentive to learning about other churches and the history and content of Catholic relations with them.[24]

Staff Selection and Development

Administrators also oversee the hiring of faculty for the Catholic schools. Directors of religious education recruit and sometimes hire catechists. These leaders need to be particularly sensitive to the backgrounds of prospective teachers in schools and catechists in the parish. They need to work carefully to see that there is strong ownership of the school's mission or the parishes' Catholic commitments.

> All those who minister within the Catholic school by word and example assist those in their care to open their minds to grasp God's truth, their hearts to accept God's love, their hands to serve God's poor. They guide the young to appreciate their lives, cultivate their talents and share their gifts as unique persons who have been and are being loved and liberated by the Lord of life. The student can be enlightened and encouraged by the quality of unconditional care manifested in the words and deeds, life and lifestyle of the truly committed educator in the Catholic schools.[25]

Most mission statements will not be so detailed as to give specifics on the ecumenical dimension of the school's mission. Nevertheless, faculty need to be selected, whether Catholic or not, who are sympathetic to the vision of visible unity articulated by the Church and are supportive of a faith environment where reconciliation and deepening relationships among the churches is a priority. Hiring for mission is an integral part of the administrative challenge.

Selecting and preparing catechists is an even more challenging administrative responsibility. Catechist certification requirements should have an ecumenical component. Formation programs should be designed so that the Catholic commitment to unity, Catholic ecumenical principles, and the progress made since the Council are made available to the volunteer catechists.

For these religious educators, catching the spirit of the Church's ecumenical commitment and knowing where to find the text books, the ecumenical *Directory* or ecumenical documents may be all that can be expected when a new catechist begins his or her ministry. As New York Archdiocesan policy notes:

> The school principal is responsible for making clear, the importance of religious instruction, the quality of the catechetical experience in the school, the value attached to religious instruction, and the amount of time spent on religious education. Faculty, parents and students must perceive religion as the most important element of Catholic education.[26]

We would not hire a teacher or select a catechist who sees Catholicism as just another denomination. Likewise, we would not recruit an educator who was not open to and interested in deepening communion among Christians and their churches. Faculty who are not Catholic will need to understand Catholic commitments to Christian unity and dialogue. More will be said about how this might be done in Chapter VI.

Teachers who do not specialize in religion or serve on campus ministry teams in Catholic schools may not follow the Church's developments with other churches. However, they should have a supportive ecumenical spirit and be equipped by staff development programs to be receptive to the steps that are taken with other churches to build that communion for which we pray. Parish catechists especially need to be attentive to the ecumenical program of the parish so as to be able to engage parents and their students in these when possible.

Studies show an increasing number of Catholics seeing the Church as just one more option in the plethora of religious choices.[27] In this situation we need a community committed together to strengthen the religious identity of students, teachers and parents. Catholic education will touch their hearts with a love for the Church as well as insuring that they have a certain quantity of religious knowledge.

It is increasingly important to recognize that primary

evangelization may be as important in Catholic educational programming as catechetical content. The unity of the churches is not served by a culture of tolerance, indifference and religious neutrality. Neither is Catholic identity served by developing the faith in contrast with fellow Christians with whom we share so much and to whom we are committed in the pilgrimage toward visible unity.

It will be important for any school to have a core of committed Catholic administrators and teachers. Selecting non-Catholic applicants will necessitate a careful discernment, emphasizing the mission of the school, the ecumenical openness of the Christian candidate and the prospects for their ecumenical formation, relative to the Catholic Church:

> It would seem, all things being equal, that a school would place a priority on hiring the Catholic applicant when one considers the nature and purpose of Catholic education.
>
> However, in deciding upon a course of action in particular cases, the person's academic and professional backgrounds as well as his or her willingness to accept and implement the philosophy and goals of the school would be important considerations. If the school is to fulfill its mission, those on the faculty must be as prepared as possible to assist the youth to achieve an integration of culture and faith and a synthesis of faith and life.[28]

Most seasoned administrators have experiences of serious and zealous Christians who have been able to contribute more to the vibrant faith community, than some less-engaged faculty or staff who happen to have come from a culturally Catholic background.

In schools that have other Christian communities represented, it will be important that the faculty know the churches of our non-Catholic students and faculty. Occasionally, other Christians will join parish religious education programs, out of interest or because of family ties. These fellow Christians should feel welcome, their faith and church respected and their relationship to Catholicism fostered without proselytism.[29] All Christian students should understand their presence as an opportunity for ecumenical learning and fostering unity among the churches to which they belong. All attempts to undermine the Christian faith of students or faculty or any use of the school for proselytism is to be avoided.[30]

Recruiting educators for the mission proper to the parish or school is an important challenge for the administrator. We are as serious about the recruiting and selection of Catholic school religion teachers or parish catechists as we are of physics or German teachers in schools. Parish religious educators and the Catholic school teachers are on the front lines of the Church's mission of handing on the faith.

There are some Catholics who still see individual conversion to the Church as the goal of their relationship with other Christians. Of course, some individuals will seek to join the Catholic Church because of their experience in Catholic schools and their understanding of the truth of the Catholic faith. However, the Catholic Church approaches other churches with respect, seeking unity with them through dialogue, and recognizing the saving character of these communities and their sacred rituals. While individual decisions will be made, in full religious liberty, care should be taken that the Catholic school does not provide undue pressure, through peer pressure, financial incentive, or faculty enticement to change churches.

Policies and Programs

There are a variety of areas in which school and parish policies will want to take into account the Catholic ecumenical commitments.

The late Archbishop James Lyke, OFM, when he was pastor in an African American community, did not allow students or parents from the school to enter into the RCIA or become Catholics during the student's time in the school. There is always a concern that joining the Church should not be motivated by peer pressure, but by faith. It is important for those coming into full communion with the Catholic Church to do so out of conviction and in response to the call of God's grace. The parish religion program and the Catholic school curriculum should be clear about the faith and values we share, and the challenge to resolve differences, that Christians will deepen their commitment to their faith, their Church and the ecumenical mandate all Christians share from Christ.

Engaging in theological dialogue is not something that can be done easily in a school wide or parish religious education context. However, major ecumenical events can be celebrated and noted in the school and parish. For example, on the occasion of the Pope's visits to a country like Greece or Sweden, local educational administrators can have an Orthodox priest or a Lutheran pastor visit the school or religious education program. An ecumenical service can be celebrated for the student body or catechetical community to mark the event. The 1999 signing of the *Joint Declaration on Justification*, or its October anniversary, can be an opportunity for a celebration in prayer and recognition of how differently we see the Reformation today, as a result of these forty years of dialogue.

For young people, the study of theological events must be adapted to their level of understanding, and the events and the perspective on other churches can be celebrated liturgically. They can be helped to see themselves as integral to historic moments on the path to reconciliation. In neighborhoods where there are particular tensions among Christians, it is important for students to be exposed to respectful and ecumenical leaders from those communities where relationships are most difficult.

Even with competent catechists and teachers, the results of the dialogues are so profuse, theologically technical, and diverse that it would be difficult for the normal teacher to keep up with them. More materials need to be developed that make these results "teacher friendly." Teachers' guides and catechetical materials need to draw on the results of these dialogues and on the history of these ecumenical relationships.

Workshops and staff development can be of some help. In assisting a parish or school community to keep up with the life and ministry of the Church, it will be important to have in-service opportunities to review the Catholic ecumenical commitments, especially as they impact the particular situation of the community involved. Since ecumenical dialogue is a pilgrimage toward visible unity, the results of dialogues and new decisions are continually being made between the churches. These stages along the way need to be celebrated in Catholic schools and parishes.

For all staff, parish or school, it will be important to know about the local religious culture including its ecumenical component. It will be important to avoid the sort of diffuse Christianity where the particular commitments of the Catholic Church and other Christian communities are not clear. This sort of confusion is no service to the ecumenical vision of the Church in passing on the Catholic faith. Peter Phan notes, "while intra-Christian [ecumenical] and interreligious dialogue is imperative for contemporary Christian theology and practice, it is neither feasible nor productive in religious education to aim at the formation of a generically Christian attitude and identity, since it is only through a particular community of faith, with its own beliefs, rituals and ethical and spiritual practices that a person gains access to and is socialized into the common Christian heritage."[31] There is no real ecumenism without a robust and self-confident commitment to Catholicism to bring to the dialogue table.

On the other hand, some would prefer to see the commitment to unity and to other churches as an add-on, after "Catholic formation" is complete. The Catholic Church considers itself irrevocably committed to the pilgrimage toward Christian unity. Therefore, Catholics from the very beginning of their formation need to know about their bonds with fellow Christians not in the Catholic Church and that the Church is committed to dialogue with them with the hope of eventual full communion. To delay ecumenical formation for Catholics makes about as much sense as those who would want only Latin in the liturgy for young people until they had mastered an understanding of the Mass. There is no richer way to deepen one's appreciation of your own community than in sharing its gifts with others.

Where there is a campus ministry in the school, the campus minister has an important role to play in the service of the ecumenical mission of the school. The ecumenical *Directory* explicitly recommends "encounters and discussions [that] can usefully be organized with other Christians," including "meetings with students of other churches and ecclesial communities." In this sort of experiential learning "the necessity for gradualness and adaptation is very important and unavoidable." Campus ministers can provide bible studies, common prayer services and even dialogue on specific ecumenical issues, depending on the age and capacity of the students. There also may be occasions for faith sharing and common prayer among Christian faculty and youth ministers of different traditions.

Ecumenical collaboration and placement is significant in service projects. Catechists working in confirmation preparation or RCIA mystagogia have particular opportunities for engendering ecumenical experiences. Reflection on the ecumenical implications, for the Catholic Church, is an important dimension of both spiritual formation and theological reflection on ecumenical service projects.

Likewise, the school and catechetical program are the places where students and staff learn to differentiate between press reports about Catholicism and fellow Christians and the reality for which the churches stand in faith, public witness and their relationships with one another. Each cultural context differs: "ecumenical formation requires a pedagogy that is adapted to the concrete situation of the life of persons."[32]

Each school and parish will need to focus on the needs and context of the students, the churches that are in the community, as well as the faith and ecumenical program of the universal Church.

Every bishop is directed to appoint an ecumenical officer in his diocese to help promote ecumenism among the Catholics of the diocese. Many dioceses will have an ecumenical commission, composed of Catholic leaders charged with assisting parishes, schools and other elements of the diocese in pursuing the ecumenical mission of the Church. In our educational work we can take advantage of the support of the diocesan ecumenical officers. Educators should be willing to provide teachers and skilled catechists to serve on the diocesan ecumenical commission. Being attentive to the local parish and diocesan situation will also entail promoting the relationships, covenants and conciliar ecumenical programs of the diocese. School policies will take account of diocesan ecumenical policies.

Every school and parish is different. There are different religious communities in the neighborhoods and schools. There are different resources in the school and parish staffs. Therefore, there are creative, new programs, relationships and models that can be developed locally that can serve the wider Church. The school and parish have important roles in serving the bishop and the Church in developing new ecumenical relationships and models. For example, two congregations can develop an ecumenical prayer service or Lenten bible study that can go up on the diocesan website for other parishes to use. A creative teacher may devise a particular curriculum which helps teachers and students learn about a particular dialogue or relationship. Both the ecumenical *Directory* and the Holy Father's encyclical reinforce the importance of local initiatives and the gift of local experiences to the Church universal.

Many parishes and schools become creative and imaginative laboratories for ecumenical relationships and formation. Just to cite an example, many former Mother Houses of religious communities have now become conference centers. Many of these Catholic conference centers host a multiplicity of Christian congregations and ecumenical ministries which make retreats there. Some also host parishes of other denominations for worship and administrative offices. These shared facilities provide opportunities for shared spiritual experiences for Catholic classes and parish groups with other Christian communities.

Sacramental Policies

The administration of Catholic schools and religious education programs will also be sensitive to the Catholic position on sacramental sharing, since it is often in the context of school or catechetical liturgies, retreats, funerals and programs for parents that the question, especially of Eucharistic sharing, arises. How we share the mystery of the Eucharist is related to our understanding of the common baptism we share, the mystery of the Church and its unity, and the levels of communion in faith that have developed.

Some would like to reduce this question to a blanket prohibition of any sacramental sharing, or to an unreflective open hospitality. However, the ecclesial position of the Catholic is more complex. Canon Law and the ecumenical *Directory* outline a process of discernment and faith criteria for arriving at a decision. **What better place than a Catholic school or catechetical program to become educated about the depths of the mystery of the Eucharist in the Church and its implications in ecumenical practice?**

All of the Christian churches recognize two principles about the celebration of the Eucharist: 1) it represents ecclesial communion in Christ, and therefore is a sign of church unity among those who receive; and 2) it is a means for building up ecclesial unity among baptized Christians. Some churches emphasize one or the other of the principles in a different balance than the Catholic Church. These two basic principles are taken into account together, as the *Directory* notes, therefore:

> …in general the Catholic Church permits access to its Eucharistic communion and to the sacraments of penance and anointing of the sick, only to those who share its oneness in faith, worship and ecclesial life. For the same reasons, it also recognizes that in certain circumstances, by way of exception, and under certain conditions, access to these sacraments may be permitted, or even commended, for Christians of other Churches and ecclesial Communities.[33]

It is important that the parish catechetical program and Catholic school be places where these principles are known, and their particular application in the local diocese is recognized. These two principles present particular tension, especially as we proceed on the road toward full sacramental communion. It is also important to realize that the application of these principles may vary from one diocese to another. In some countries, the episcopal conference may have interpretations of the guidelines which apply to all the dioceses, but in the United States each diocese may have its own that can differ from one diocese to another.

Because the Catholic Church recognizes the priestly ministry and therefore the full Eucharistic mystery of the Orthodox, Eastern and Oriental, the Assyrian Church of the East and Polish National Catholics in North America, Eucharistic sharing is possible when pastorally necessary.

While the Catholic Church may be open to sacramental sharing, these churches do not allow for Catholics to receive in their churches or for their members to receive from Roman Catholic priests. The Syrian [Oriental] Orthodox, the Polish National Catholic, and the Assyrian Church of the East are exceptions. The Orthodox emphasize the first of the two principles, that Eucharist is a sign of unity existing or achieved. Common Declarations between Pope John Paul II and the Syrian and Assyrian Patriarchs have opened the way for sacramental sharing when pastorally warranted. The Polish National Catholic Church in North America has been judged by the Holy See to be in the same situation as the Eastern churches in this matter.

The issue with the various communities of the Reformation is more complex, but not less important in the context of a school or parish faith community. Catholics never receive penance or Eucharist in these churches because we have not yet resolved issues of ordained ministry, or fully recognized their sacramental celebrations, though we do recognize their sacred, grace-giving character. Catholics and Anglicans claim the same doctrine of holy orders, but we still have not resolved the questions of the ordination of women. With the Lutherans and some other Protestants there are developed dialogues on the sacrament of order, and we recognize that God uses their ministers in the work of the church, but we have not reached a level of agreement where sacramental recognition and sharing would be possible. With some of them, like Lutheran and Anglican, we have developed substantial agreement on the meaning of the Eucharist. However, our ability to share communion with them awaits full reconciliation in one ordained ministry. As Catholics, we don't use the language "intercommunion," because we believe that we are either in Eucharistic communion or we are not. From a Catholic and Orthodox point of view, sacramental communion is intimately related to communion in one Church.

Occasions when members of these churches can receive at a Catholic Mass, by way of pastoral exception, require more discernment – a general invitation or a general prohibition is not prescribed. The *Directory*, again, is very specific:

Catholic ministers will judge individual cases and administer these sacraments only in accord with these [diocesan or episcopal conference] established norms, where they exist. Otherwise they will judge according to the norms of this *Directory*.

The conditions under which a Catholic minister may administer the sacraments of the Eucharist, of penance and of the anointing of the sick to a baptized person who may be found in the circumstances given above are that the person be unable to have recourse for the sacrament desired to a minister of his or her own Church or ecclesial Community, ask for the sacrament of his or her own initiative, manifest Catholic faith in this sacrament and be properly disposed.[34]

For example, Episcopal or Protestant parents will often ask whether Eucharistic sharing is appropriate at a first communion or confirmation. Decisions about such questions will require a discussion, and where necessary, the consultation with appropriate diocesan leadership. As the *Directory* itself notes, interchurch families provide a context that is itself an exceptional one and requires special pastoral attentiveness.

The application of the norms can vary from diocese to diocese, according to the pastoral needs of the situation and the judgment of the local bishop.

This is true across the globe in different episcopal conferences. For example, South Africa and the episcopal conferences of Britain and Ireland have issued guidelines, and the episcopal conference of the United States has not, though many dioceses have done so.[35] Some reserve the individual decision to the bishop or his ecumenical commission, others leave it in the hands of the individual presenting him or herself and the local Catholic minister, within the guidelines of the *Directory*.

A Catholic school or catechetical administrator, especially those with other Christians in the faculty and student body or among the parents, will do well to know not only the general Catholic position, but also the disposition of the local bishop. In the school or catechetical context it is often possible for the elements of peer pressure and cultural relations between church groups to have an influence that can tend to override the understandings of the churches and their sacraments.

It may be important to help other Christians in Catholic programs to find parallel opportunities in their own churches, for example, for first communion or confirmation. It may even be appropriate for classes to follow these important ritual moments, without sacramental sharing, with prayers for the day when full communion is restored.

If proper instruction is lacking, for students and parents, or if the position of the non-Catholic's church is not understood and taken seriously, there can be occasion for misunderstanding and tension. However, these occasions should be, rather "teachable moments" where the history of division is made clear, the steps and commitment toward healing these tensions is laid out, and the hunger for sacramental sharing is engendered.

Some Christian churches, for example the Orthodox on one side and the Methodists on the other, have an understanding of the Church and its Eucharistic practice that varies from Catholic faith and practice. All concerned students, staff and administration need to understand these points of view and devise a pedagogical strategy that is both pastorally sensitive and educationally effective. While Catholics should be instructed that in appropriate circumstances Orthodox will be welcome to communion at a Catholic Mass, or Catholics would be free to go to communion in an Orthodox Liturgy, because of Orthodox understanding of the Church, we do not go to communion nor do we encourage Orthodox students at Mass to receive communion which is contrary to the discipline of their churches. If we happen to be at Methodist Church, all Christians are routinely welcomed to come to communion. However, Catholics should know that it is not appropriate for them to go to the table, and that no pressure should be put on them to do so. If the varieties of points of view are learned in catechetical programs, it will enable more comfortable participation in one another's worship without embarrassment.

Some Christians announce that all who believe in Jesus Christ and repent of their sins are welcome to the Lord's Table. We do not practice this "open communion," but we understand the faith on which it is based and respect the churches that practice it. Presbyterians, Methodists and Disciples consider the Eucharist the Lord's Table and an occasion for deepening the communion among Christians. Therefore, they always invite all Christians present to receive, while respecting the fact that Catholics, Orthodox and some Protestants are not free to do so because of the link they draw between unity of the Church and unity at the Lord's Table. Episcopalians and Lutherans allow all who are baptized, in good standing with their own church, believe in the real presence of Christ, and are properly disposed to come forward to receive. Christians from these churches do not always understand Catholic and Orthodox faith and practice, and therefore should be provided the educational resources to do so.

We do not prohibit all sacramental sharing, but we observe the practices of the churches that do prohibit it, and do not put pressure on their members to receive communion with us, even though it is permitted in our understanding of the Church. Orthodox, except for the Syrian Church of Antioch, do not permit sacramental sharing until full communion is restored, though exceptions may be made in pastoral emergencies. While it would be permitted for members of these (Orthodox) churches to receive at a Catholic Mass if properly disposed and in spiritual need, we do not encourage individuals to do so in violation of the faith and practice of their own churches. It will be important to instruct them and their Catholic peers, when there are Orthodox in our catechetical and school programs.

In many communities where ecumenical relationships are well developed and Christians understand one another's Eucharistic practice, the individual who is unable to communicate at a Eucharist of another church will go up and receive a blessing. The Holy Father was very moved when the Archbishop of Uppsala in Sweden came forward for such a blessing on the Pope's visit there. In England, the Cardinal of Westminster will receive a blessing from the Archbishop of Canterbury during an Anglican liturgy and the Archbishop will come forward for a blessing from the Cardinal during Catholic Mass.

These and other administrative sensitivities and initiatives are all part of what is appropriate in formation of teachers and catechists. In some locales, there may be some reasons for school administrative positions to be limited to Catholics. However, other Christians may also be considered if they are equipped with the vision and commitments of Catholic education, including its ecumenical resources, hopes and practices.

Administrative initiatives:
- Common prayer, Week of Prayer (usually in January), etc.
- Ecumenical Faith Community Formation
- Recruiting faculty, catechists, and administration for Mission, including unity
- In-service ecumenical formation
- Ecumenically informed Catholic curriculum
- Ecumenical service projects and reflection
- Diocesan collaboration in ecumenical programming

- Celebrations and experiences of dialogue and events
- Ecumenically informed school/catechetical policies
- Knowledge and sensitivity to ecumenical environment and cultures in which students and faculty live.

A major element in securing the Catholic identity of the school and within all students is to assure that catechists and religion faculty are selected so as to join a core of mission oriented colleagues on school or parish religious education staff. However, the religious dimension of the Catholic school and its ecumenical program cannot be relegated to the religion faculty. All teachers need to be effective in their relational skills, and be able to touch the hearts of their students. There are always students for whom the relational dimension of the Gospel will be more important, at certain moments in their development, than the cognitive content of the tradition.

The catechists in religious education programs and the mission oriented faculty in Catholic schools are especially attentive to those alienated from the faith because of family, developmental stage, or personal conviction. This evangelical spirit should be characteristic of a wider circle in school and parish than those who teach religion.

Those involved in the catechetical task are challenged to "...assume an 'ecumenical dimension' everywhere." (GDC 197) This means that, while engendering a love for Christ, and a loyalty and affection for the Church, catechists are also called as Pope John Paul II reminds us, to awaken a zeal for the unity of the Church. The catechists' role is to motivate students so that they are awakened to a zeal for the unity of the churches. They engender a desire to understand other churches. This understanding will enable young people to grow into a world where they can work with fellow Christians.

Cultural Differences

In specific ethnic communities, ecumenical catechesis will take on appropriate cultural forms. We will give only two examples here, but parallels within Eastern European, Irish, Southern-Evangelical, upper Midwest-Lutheran, and other cultural contexts can be developed as appropriate.

In the Hispanic communities, new arrivals often do not have the experience of pluralism and the habit of living with fellow Christians, characteristic of those who have lived and related to other churches for generations. They may find Pentecostal and other evangelical Christians more hospitable and providing more Christian outreach than their Catholic parishes. They will need to be welcomed, provided with a strong grounding in their Catholic identity and helped in understanding the variety of Christian groups among whom they will live their Christian faith.[36]

In nurturing African American Catholic ecumenism, sensitivity will be needed regarding the history of exclusion. The African American community is often characterized by the predominance of Protestant culture. Their ministers have an important role in community and political life. In this community ecumenical priority is given to common witness against racism and for justice. Catholic catechesis will affirm the African American heritage and the core elements of the faith shared with African American Protestants, but for Catholic students it will also emphasize the sacramental and ecclesiological elements that are unique to our Catholic heritage.

Catechetical Renewal

When we moved to a renewed catechetical model on the eve of the Council, much of our kerygmatic, liturgical and biblical catechetical principles were supported by the Council documents. However, little did we know the challenges we would face in these 40 years of catechetical renewal. Since the Council, catechesis has inculturated in a variety of contexts. Catholic editorial houses and presses and catechetical centers have made an important contribution to the renewal of religion teaching, well before the resources of the Catechetical Directories and the *Catechism of the Catholic Church* were developed to help them.

A key element in the program of Catholic renewal is the contribution of the ecumenical dialogues and the teaching of the Magisterium. While texts and curricula are supportive of the Catholic educator, both the educator and the resources used need to be informed by the best principles of ecumenical formation the Catholic Church can provide. The steps we have taken toward deepening communion among Christians have been among the most exciting harvests of the conciliar vision of the Church. Their implications for our catechesis have been rich and challenging.

The basis of the Catholic school and parish catechetical program is a fully integrated curriculum with the Catholic heritage having pride of place among the subjects taught in the Catholic school:

> Above all they [students] should know their own Church and be able to give an account of her teaching, her discipline and her principles of ecumenism. The more they know these, the better they can present them in discussions with other Christians and give sufficient reason for them. They should also have accurate knowledge of the other Churches and ecclesial Communities with whom they are in contact. Careful note must be taken of the various prerequisites for ecumenical engagement that are set out in the Decree on Ecumenism of the Second Vatican Council.[37]

The "prerequisites for ecumenical engagement" will be spelled out below as they apply to different aspects of Catholic education in schools and parishes. The Holy Father is particularly concerned that catechists take their role in incorporating the results of ecumenical progress into Catholic instruction. "At the stage which we have now reached, this process of mutual enrichment must be taken seriously into account... a new task lies before us: that of receiving the results already achieved" which "must involve the whole people of God." Results are not to remain "statements of bilateral commissions, but must become a common heritage."[38]

Before students can fully assimilate these results coming from forty years of dialogue at the highest levels, catechists will want to know what has been done and then help adapt these results to the age levels and learning styles of students and the specific contexts.

Elements of Ecumenical Catechesis

Catechesis carries a particularly important role in both imparting knowledge and forming a "genuine ecumenical attitude." The Directory outlines five elements of importance in the ecumenical dimension of catechesis: a) providing solid doctrinal content taught within an understanding of the "hierarchy of truths," b) teaching about other churches honestly, recognizing them as means of salvation, c) helping students purify themselves and nourishing them in a true desire for unity, d) prepare young and maturing Catholics for living with other Christians, and e) keeping a clear perspective on the distinctions between the truths of faith and their expression.[39] These elements are echoed in the *General Directory for Catechesis*. (¶ 197, 198)

Among the most important segments of the Catholic curriculum for ecumenical content and sensitivity is that on spiritual ecumenism, rooted in common baptism and expressing the real, if imperfect, communion among all Christians. The fourth chapter of the ecumenical *Directory*, "Communion in Life and Spiritual Activity Among the Baptized," needs to inform any sacramental catechesis. It not only outlines Catholic priorities in spiritual ecumenism, but it also details the understanding and practice of sacramental sharing, especially Eucharist and marriage.

As we know, when we have students studying the sacraments and especially marriage, they are not often energized by the implications of our faith in the sacrament and its implications for life. On the other hand, when couples present themselves for marriage today, they are generally not so very disposed to move into a learning mode. In fact, increasingly marriage preparation becomes an opportunity as much for primary evangelization for Catholics whose affiliation with the Church and the knowledge of its faith has weakened, as it is for a catechesis on marriage.

It is especially challenging to prepare young people for the issues to be faced in interchurch marriages when they are not of the marrying age or are not involved with other Christians personally. For this reason, catechesis on interchurch marriage and the Catholic vision is as important as catechesis on the Eucharist and its role in ecumenical reconciliation.

If the results of the dialogues in which the Catholic Church has been involved over the last forty years are to become a common heritage, as the Holy Father suggests, they must find ways of touching our curricula at all levels. The Holy See, through the Pontifical Council for Promoting Christian Unity, and many episcopal conferences around the world, have entered into dialogue with many churches: Orthodox, Anglican, historic Protestant, Pentecostal, Evangelical and the like.

The careful biblical and historical research has healed many differences on issues like Scripture and tradition, the Eucharist and ordained ministry, baptism and the nature of the church, church and authority, marriage, ethics, and the saints and Mary. However, these are technical texts with a variety of levels of agreement. The task is now before the educational communities to find ways of making these remarkable results part of the mainstream of Catholic life through its catechetical programs and new lived relationships.

We are fortunate to have major results of dialogues with other churches gathered in research volumes that are available for school and parish libraries.[40] However, these technical theological resources, as rich as they are, need to be translated into "teacher friendly" resources in text books, study guides and teachers' manuals to accompany every element of the Catholic religious curriculum.

There are some text materials emerging that can be used in the formation of religion teachers and provide resources for administrators and board members.[41] However, the urgency with which the Holy Father speaks of reception requires more ecumenically informed catechetical materials adapted for every level of Catholic education.

The pertinent dialogue results must find their way into teachers' guides. When teaching the sacraments, teachers need to know with which churches we have substantial agreement, which are in dialogue to resolve issues, and which do not have a sacramental understanding of the Church and even rebaptize Catholics. When teaching grace and the Reformation, the fact that Lutherans and Catholics hold the same faith and no longer condemn one another over the issue that was central to the Reformation: Justification – grace and good works – now colors all we teach both on Christian history and God's gracious love in Jesus Christ.

Ecumenical Formation emphasizes three principles in Catholic formation: 1) interpretation, 2) the hierarchy of truths, and 3) the importance of the results of the dialogues becoming a common heritage. We have discussed the third point in some detail.

Principles for Ecumenical Catechesis

1) Catechetics needs to interpret scripture and Church history, and the Christian Tradition within it, in reconciling ways. Thus Paul's admonition to the Corinthians (I Cor. 1), and the apostles meeting in the Council of Jerusalem (Acts 15) are evidences of the ecumenical spirit from the very beginning of the Church. The variety of witnesses in the bible: the four Gospels, the different approaches Paul takes to the variety of local churches, and the variety of forms of ministry, all point to the unity in diversity that characterizes the Christian community.

Ecumenical agreements give us new lenses through which to read the texts of the Councils and tragic moments of Christian history, like the early councils (431, 451), the alienation of East and West and the Reformation, moments of estrangements which are beginning to be healed in the last decades of the 20th century and the beginning of the new millennium.

2) The hierarchy of truths is not about more and less important matters of faith, but rather about the relationships of what we believe to the core revelation of God in Jesus Christ. For example, our belief in Mary and her role in redemption relates to our belief in the saving role of Christ in the mystery of salvation. All belief about the Most Blessed Virgin is faith about Christ and what he has done in his saving work for the Church, first among whose members is Mary, the Mother of God.

Catechists distinguish between what is necessary for Catholics to believe and private devotions which may be popular in Catholic life, but do not constitute the core of the faith. While the Church encourages devotions, whether private or liturgical, the Council admonishes against excess or confusion among the faithful. Christian faith, on the other hand, requires belief in Mary's role as the Mother of God.

We share with Protestant, Orthodox and Anglican Christians the belief in the role of Mary as Mother of God. These churches do not share our convictions about the Immaculate Conception or the Assumption being dogmas necessary for salvation. Many believe them as did Luther. In explaining them to Catholic students and to fellow Christian educators in other churches, it is important to note that the Immaculate Conception is about God's grace being given to Mary prior to any action of her own. Its focus is primarily on the Incarnation and on God's initiative. The Assumption is about God's commitment to all of us, recognizing our Lady as the first fruits of our common resurrection in Christ.

There are many and rich devotions in the Church, sometimes even competitive with one another and appearing to others as more important than even our Eucharistic liturgical life. It is important for Catholic catechesis and for communication with fellow Christians to note the centrality of the faith as what binds Catholics together in our understanding of Mary. Within that common faith, a wide variety of devotions or none at all are possible.

As liturgical, biblical and Eucharistic renewal deepens and catechesis helps our people differentiate between what is required in faith and what is permitted in devotion, Catholic perspectives on Mary will become a clearer witness to Gospel balance. Catholics will not expect, as we move more closely together, Orthodox and Protestant devotion to take on the same form as Catholics, anymore than there is devotional uniformity among Catholics worldwide.

Catholic catechesis at its best will incorporate the results of Catholic dialogues with other churches, an interpretive perspective which will show a historical understanding of the Catholic faith and a positive approach to other churches, and an exposition of the faith taking account of the "hierarchy of truths." It will teach skills of collaboration and dialogue. It will be clear on Catholic self understanding and the Church's priority for and principles of ecumenism. Above all, it will seek to touch the hearts of the Catholic community with a conversion toward the Gospel imperative of reconciliation. If zeal for unity is stirred up in the heart, as commitment to Christ and his will for the Church, the information can be acquired as one develops in the faith according to the age and styles of learning of the individual.

Eastern Churches

Western, Latin Catholics need to know of the variety of Eastern Churches in communion with Rome. These used to be spoken of as "rites." Since the Eastern Code of Canon Law, 1991, they are called "churches *sui juris* (with their own legal tradition)" which have their own synodical governance, their own proper spirituality, law, liturgy and theology.[42]

While these relationships are not properly ecumenical since Catholics of both Latin and Eastern traditions are in full communion, catechetical programs need to foster an understanding and appreciation of these churches, in addition to the Latin Church, that make up the Catholic Church.

Appreciation of the history and attendance at the liturgy of these churches are important parts of our catechesis. It will be helpful for teachers to recognize the tensions they have with both Latin Catholics with whom they are in full communion, and with the Orthodox whose traditions they share. Again, students and catechists will learn about these fellow Catholics better by visiting them and hearing from their teachers and clergy directly.

Knowledge of national background and ethnicity are important factors in understanding the Eastern Churches, Catholic and Orthodox. Each of these churches has a particular cultural history that is a gift to its liturgical, spiritual and ethical tradition, but can also be a burden that isolates the community from other Christians.

Ethical Formation in an Ecumenical Context

Differences on ethical issues are a challenge to our Christian charity and to a catechesis grounded on the fundamental unity we share in Christ. This is especially true when these issues are polarizing in the public political environment. Catholics with their ecumenical partners have produced important sets of principles that can be useful in our catechesis on divisive ethical issues.

It is important to clarify for our students and catechists the tremendous common ground we share even when we seem to differ so dramatically in our public policy witness. Dialogues with the Reformed on human rights and abortion and with the Methodists on end of life issues are important resources in our prolife catechesis, delineating common approaches and differences.

Keeping abreast of Catholic ecumenical developments is important for the catechist and religious education leadership. Resources from both the Magisterium and from the dialogues are rich. However, the constantly evolving relationships among Christians, and the variety of situations in which our Catholic people live make it essential that there be opportunities for periodic updating and review of these relationships and their relevance for our educational styles and content.

Catechetical Challenges

1) What are the challenges in your ministry for engendering a commitment to the Church and to its ecumenical outreach?

2) What are the catechetical strategies most helpful in eliciting commitment to the Church and its goal of unity with other Christians?

3) What are the tensions that young people and adults experience around understanding of and commitment to the Church, its specificity and its goal of unity with other Christians?

4) What have been the most positive ecumenical resources for communicating and engendering the Church's understanding of and commitment to unity? What are resources that are most needed in this dimension of our catechetical work?

The Parish Directors of Religious Education

The evolving role of the Parish Director of Religious Education has been one of the major elements in Catholic education in the last thirty years. This is a professional position, like the school principal or president, the university dean or the pastoral associate, that provides both an opportunity for ecclesial lay ministry and a challenge as one of the pillars of parish administration.

Often the DRE has responsibilities that touch on the school and the Rite of Christian Initiation for Adults, as well as the parish school of religion for adults and for young people not in the Catholic parochial schools. Liturgy formation and marriage preparation are sometimes connected with the work of the parish DRE. This role will be increasingly important in the identity and style of parish leadership as the Catholic Church moves into the twenty first century.

The DRE's work in parish formation entails the conversion of church leadership and of catechists. Conversion is central to all ecumenical efforts. The catechists who are under the leadership of the DRE will need to be awakened to the vision of Christian unity. Some may come to their volunteer ministry well disposed or even well formed in the ecumenical dimension to the Catholic faith. For others, special attention may be necessary for this dimension of their formation.

The catechists will need to come to an understanding of Catholic ecumenical principles. It will be important for them to understand the churches with which Catholics relate. They will develop the skills to serve the Church's ecumenical mission. (GCD 29, 53-57, 56-57)

DREs must acquire ecumenical experience, an ecumenical spirituality, and sufficient knowledge of ecumenical developments to lead catechists and to help them provide a context for students in following Christ on this ecumenical pilgrimage.

Criteria have been developed by the National Conference on Catechetical Leadership for the parish DRE that assist both the DRE and his or her colleagues to assess the strengths and needs of the persons who hold this important position. There are also, now, resources that have been provided by the National Conference of Catechetical Leadership to equip the DRE for their role, including a special volume on meeting the ecumenical dimensions of their responsibilities and criteria.[43]

Formation for DREs varies widely. Many come with rich ecumenical experience and fine academic formation. Others are seasoned catechists whose formation is provided through years of in-service work and occasional formal programs. Still others are career ecclesial lay ministers who have chosen this field from amid the many vocations to which they might have responded in the Church. All of these vocational journeys provide resources that can enrich the parish educational life. However, attention must also be given to enrich the background of the DRE and especially the volunteer catechists who provide the core of Catholic education in many parishes. Regular updating for the DREs and for the parish catechists will be essential to the diocesan and parish programming.

While the DRE may not be involved in all of the sacramental programs in a parish, he or she carries a particularly important leadership role in knowing where the Catholic Church is on these matters and how the various sacramental catechetical programs serve the common vision of the parish and total Catholic education in the Church.

The DRE can ask the diocesan director of ecumenism to come or send a representative to team up with a member of the other church in explaining where the dialogue is with that particular church, in the diocese and around the world. In some parishes and dioceses there are covenant relationships with particular congregations or denominations. The DRE can help the catechists make these relationships part of the prayer life and catechetical program in a special way. The Catholic Church sponsors a host of dialogues with different ecumenical partners, noted earlier.

The dialogues between Episcopalians and Lutherans are best known among Catholics. However, it will be important also to review the other Protestant churches, especially since the Methodist and Baptist communities are the largest churches in the United States.

Sensitivity to, and knowledge about, Pentecostal, Holiness, and evangelical fellow Christians in the local community and outreach to them is important, as well as knowing the difference from the Mormons and Jehovah's Witnesses whom we do not consider Christians in the classical sense. Above all, students need to know the difference between these churches and the churches to which Catholics are committed together on the pilgrimage toward full communion.

The "teacher friendly" guides to the ecumenical results of bilateral and multilateral dialogues have yet to be written. In the meantime, the DRE is an important colleague with the parish ecumenical representative and the diocesan ecumenical officer in helping the fruits of theological conversation become for our parishes, as the Holy Father says, "a common heritage."

Rite of Christian Initiation for Adults

The DREs who work with the *Rite of Christian Initiation for Adults* will be particularly attentive to ecumenical results as they apply to the formation of the RCIA teams and to distinguishing clearly between baptized candidates and unbaptized catechumens in catechesis proper to the RCIA process and in the celebration of the rites. While community formation will often dictate that the baptized and catechized can be grouped together in much of the process, the richness that catechized non-Catholics bring to the Church and the process of initiation needs to be acknowledged and maximized. [44]

For those candidates raised on a rich biblical Christian catechesis, presentations of the creed and the bible are not appropriate rituals, as these candidates may already be imbued with the Christian faith and the Sacred Scripture by the community in which their Christian life was nurtured. For those candidates seeking full communion who have attended Mass for years with a spouse, more attention may need to be given to how their church of origin and its worship life relate to Catholicism than to the Catholic sacramental life itself. For Christians coming with an evangelical enthusiasm for the Catholic Church, from evangelical Protestant background, nonfundamentalist Catholic ways of interpreting scripture may be essential. For Christians from denominational Protestant backgrounds, who may know the lectionary well and be comfortable with Catholic worship, the specifics of Catholic ecclesiology may be important. Finally, all coming into the Catholic Church, as new Christians or as Christians coming into full communion, will need to know the Catholic zeal for the unity of the churches and Catholic commitments to the particular churches with whom we are in dialogue.

Some dioceses have parish ecumenical representatives that relate to the ecumenical officers and commissions of the dioceses and take leadership in parish programming. The representatives, where they exist or where they can be encouraged, for example as one task within a parish council, can be a good colleague of the DRE. They can help to provide ecumenical formation for the parish catechists or ecumenical experiences for the RCIA and students in the catechetical programs. With the limited time that parish volunteer catechists, RCIA sponsors and sometimes even DREs have at their disposal for their ministry, it will be important to have parish members with special ecumenical interest and expertise contribute to this dimension of the catechetical process.

However, in many parishes up to half of those involved in the process of Christian initiation are not catechumens. Catholics are challenged to take our baptismal theology seriously. RCIA leaders need to provide the necessary ecumenical sensitivity and to bring all those in Christian initiation processes in the community into deeper contact with the mainstream of congregational and Catholic life.[45]

The Rite itself provides a special service for the reception into full communion of those who are already baptized: "This is the liturgical rite by which a person born and baptized in a separated ecclesial community is received, according to the Latin rite, into the full communion of the Catholic Church. The rite is so arranged that *no greater burden than necessary is required for the establishment of communion and unity.*"

Nevertheless, many Christians coming to the Catholic Church need as serious initiation process as the individual who has no Christian background. They need to know the distinctive claims of the Catholic faith and to understand its ecumenical mission and openness. For example, we have some Anglican and Protestant Christians with a *denominational* understanding of church that sees no need for special initiation. They only want to *transfer* into the Catholic Church as one might move from a parish in one city to another when one takes a new job. They will need to understand the sacramental, hierarchical and ecumenical character of Catholicism.

On the other hand, there are others who come from more *sectarian* even fundamentalist backgrounds who have a view of the Church that may be more rigid and literalistic than is the tradition. For these, catechists will have to help them see the openness of Catholicism to biblical scholarship, its theological and cultural inclusiveness, its social justice ministry, and its ecumenical commitments.

Christians presenting themselves for full communion with the Catholic Church will build on the faith nurtured in other communities. This may be ritualized by acknowledging the gifts the Catholic Church receives from the church of the new Catholic. Opportunities should be provided for the new Catholic to study the relationship of the Catholic Church to their previous church and the hopes or challenges we have in moving toward full communion.

Other Christians Associated with Parish Catechetical Programs

On occasion, there are Christians from other churches who participate in the religious education program of the parish. What is said above about the administration of the religious education curriculum applies equally in the classes where a Protestant or Orthodox Christian might participate.

This is particularly delicate in areas of sacramental preparation. For example, Orthodox and Eastern Catholics will have had first communion and confirmation at the time of baptism. At the time of first communion, there may be some tension because some Protestants do not celebrate first communion in their own church, and may not fully understand that Holy Communion means full initiation into the Catholic Church.

Much more common is the fellow Christian from another church who is a parent of one of the students. It will be important for parent formation programs to be sensitive to the non-Catholic parents providing special interviews if that will be helpful or even materials from the dialogues between the Catholic Church and the church to which the non-Catholic parent belongs. At times of sacramental preparation and reception, special attention needs to be given to the formation of non-Catholic family members and even friends. The DRE can also provide resources to assist dialogue within the interchurch family.

Marriage Preparation

Preparing young people to understand the sacrament of marriage and assisting couples in proximate preparation for their own marriage is an important dimension of sacramental catechesis, especially since Catholic understanding differs so markedly from the secular culture and some of the Protestant churches. In some communities, wedding preparation becomes an occasion for evangelization for the uncatechized or inactive Catholic. Sensitivity is especially important in preparing those entering into an interchurch marriage because the couple may not foresee the tensions religion can cause in child rearing or in living out an active church life with different commitments. Young people coming to marriage may do so at a time when mutual attraction may have a stronger driving force in their lives than their commitments to Church.

Couples in successful interchurch marriages are important resources in marriage preparation and in follow-up mentoring. These couples can demonstrate from their own family life how faith can be shared, while loyalty to different churches is honored. They can talk young people through the kinds of questions engaged couples either take for granted or can defer until after marriage – like the issues around baptism of children, family prayer life, or patterns of Sunday worship. There are special inventories prepared for interchurch couples that can enable them to foresee questions that come up in the religious practice after marriage and their approaches to child rearing, that can help avoid misunderstandings later.

The church needs to find ways to nurture the faith of couples in interchurch families. Often, when both spouses are active in their churches, they can become strong ecumenical leaders. Likewise, the results of the dialogues are important resources for preparing couples for an interchurch wedding if they are religiously interested and in nurturing the interchurch family. The zeal for the unity of the Church has a particular urgency in families with active members in different Christian churches.

Educational programming in the parish must be attentive to the needs of these couples and the resource they provide for ecumenical interest and spiritual nurture of other interchurch couples who may experience strains on their relationship.

It is also important to realize that Orthodox, Anglican and Protestant churches have different approaches to remarriage after the dissolution of an earlier marriage. These differences on divorce and remarriage cause a great deal of strain and anguish in some relationships. For example, when a potential spouse has to enter into an annulment process before a Catholic marriage is possible, they may find the procedure overly juridical and intrusive. Care needs to be taken that those coming into a Catholic sacramental marriage or joining the RCIA know Catholic marriage legislation and the religious foundations for it in a pastoral and sensitive way, before it becomes an obstacle.

Fortunately, there are a number of resources to assist in understanding and ministering to interchurch couples.[46] The annulment process is a difficult one for other Christians to understand, so careful catechesis and sensitivity are important when this sad necessity may arise.

Other Christian Ministers

Catholics do not yet fully recognize the ordained sacramental ministry of any of the Reformation churches. Nevertheless, we do not deny the ministerial importance and efficacy of Protestant and Anglican clergy in serving their people. We rather speak of a "defect" or "incompleteness" from our point of view, a deficiency that Catholics and Protestants are called to work together to overcome. For the fullness of the Eucharistic mystery, a priest ordained by a bishop in apostolic succession recognized by the Catholic Church is required. Only the Orthodox, Polish National Catholic and Assyrian Church of the East are now recognized as sharing these with us.

It is important for Catholic people to know ministers and priests of other Christian communities, to respect them, and to look forward to the day when we can celebrate one, united ministry around the eucharistic table.

DREs can develop supportive spiritual relationships among the educators and leaders of other traditions. When we have questions or problems, do we have colleagues and friends we can call in other churches and ask candid questions, get personal spiritual support or find resources for our catechetical ministry? Do we provide a resource for information about Catholic life, about retreats and spirituality centers or about educational programs for our Protestant and Orthodox colleagues?

In many ways, the DRE is called to juggle a variety of dimensions of parish catechetical leadership and linkages with the wider Church, Catholic and ecumenical. In some dioceses the ecumenical commission is supplemented by deanery committees and representatives, and Parish Ecumenical Representatives (PERs). These latter are important colleagues for the parish DREs in their role of promoting ecumenical formation within the parish.

The ethical dimension of the catechetical task is of particular urgency and delicacy in the contemporary American cultural context. Both our Christian tradition of social teaching, touching on the unborn, peace, justice and respect for the environment, and our teaching about personal morality, touching on sexuality, honesty and personal discipline, run quite contrary to the culture which surrounds us. Some churches and some Catholics try to isolate themselves from society to preserve a Christian environment in their formation. Others seek to find ways of both preserving our distinctive discipline and moral vision and reaching out to evangelize culture. (GDC 85-86)

Fellow Christians are important colleagues in both the moral formation of our people and in the common approaches to influencing the ethics of society around us. For the DRE, discussion with other Christian educators about their approaches to moral formation in their congregations and exploring ways of collaboration in the ethical component of catechesis will be important.

Part of Catholic education is helping catechists and students be grateful for the gifts already received from other traditions. We can open any Catholic hymnal and read through the hymns included from Charles Wesley and other non-Catholic authors. This can be a great learning experience when a catechist points students to the Methodist Church down the street, or tells the story of the Wesley brothers and their impact on spiritual renewal in Britain and the U.S.

Fellow Christians from Other Churches in Catholic Schools

Some of our Catholic schools have had dedicated Christians from other churches as part of their faculty and student body for decades. Some have developed special programs of formation parallel to the Catholic catechetical programs. Some have employed these committed fellow Christians in dimensions of the religious formation of students and faculty.

Catholic schools with a long experience of fellow Christian students and faculty can provide a rich resource of tried models for working in a pluralistic environment. Today we have resources for integrating these fellow Christians in our common search for the visible unity of the Church. Some have been very intentionally ecumenical, drawing on the resources of the Magisterium and developments since the Second Vatican Council. Others have adapted from more practical exigencies. Most of these schools and parishes in communities where Catholics are a minority have reflected for years on Catholic identity formation in a pluralistic society.

The NCEA has already provided some resources for the schools, especially for those totally Catholic schools where other Christians were a new phenomenon. In some very Catholic communities, like Boston, where old ethnic neighborhoods have given way to mixed ethnic and African American Protestant newcomers, a variety of motives have led to a transition to a more pluralistic student body and faculty.

As Monsignor James Hawker remarked of Boston's Cathedral High School:

> Although the situation at Cathedral High has evolved over the years the school has continued to exercise a truly unique and valuable service as an educational agency of the Church. This is due in large part to the willingness of the personnel therein to consider seriously the mission and responsibility of the Catholic school in relation to those persons within the school who are identified with other religious traditions and to formulate a position on the matter.[47]

As Catholic educators we partner with other Christians in passing on the Christian faith in communities and schools where we work together. For certain of our partner churches, like the African American churches (Methodist, Baptist, Holiness, Pentecostal, Independent, etc.), service of the poor and support of the faith of young people without proselytism are common tasks. Christian values are the foundation for dialogue and a lifelong commitment to unity. For these churches, our Catholic schools and parish outreach together in the community will be more important than theological agreements in creating a credible Catholic ecumenism. This grassroots educational challenge is an important mark of African American Christians which we share. For Catholics this commitment emerges from our understanding of our Church as in real, if yet imperfect, communion with other churches.

In the African American community, Catholic educators should know that the Holy See has official dialogues with the Baptist, Methodist and Pentecostal churches to which most African American Christians belong.

In receiving non-Catholic students into a Catholic school, special attention will need to be given to clarifying the mission of the school for the parents and assisting the student to understand the educational environment they are joining. Catholic schools tend to be better academic learning environments than their public school counterparts. However, prospective parents and students, Catholic or otherwise, should be invited to join in the school enterprise because of its mission of handing on the Christian faith. Catholic identity, including ecumenical commitment, must be clear to all. Catholic schools are not merely a private school alternative with superior secular standards to the public school.

High school students' interviews for incoming pupils include both students and parents, whereas the parent carries the major responsibility for elementary school students' decisions. Monsignor Hawker outlines important attitudes for students:

- The non-Catholic applicant should understand, accept and be willing to support actively the philosophy and goals of the school.
- The non-Catholic applicant should be willing to relate responsibly to the members of the school community, whether adults or students.
- The non-Catholic applicant should be willing to cultivate his or her person, talents and abilities to the extent that he or she is able.
- The non-Catholic applicant should be willing to attend religion class.
- The non-Catholic applicant should realize that he or she will be invited to attend liturgy at the school and understand the reasons for that invitation.
- The non-Catholic applicant should be willing to participate in programs of service sponsored by the school.[48]

Again, participation in religion class may depend on the particular program of the school under discussion. In some cases there will be parallel programs for the non-Catholic students.

The service programs may very well be ecumenical, as they should be for the Catholic students, as we note in the secondary section (Chapter VIII). In this case, the school may wish to be intentional about engaging ecumenical service projects which include the churches from which its student body comes. The ministers of the students or their parents may be helpful to the faculty member who has responsibility for the service program of the school in finding ecumenical service programs which incorporate their particular communities.

Providing opportunities for these discussions during the application process is important, rather than waiting until the school year has begun.

Students

Today, Catholic schools nurture the faith of their students within their own communities. That is, Christians from other churches will be encouraged to supplement their Catholic schooling with attention to the Sunday school and other programs in their congregations. The ecumenical task is one of reconciling churches and supporting one another. Common prayer and spiritual sharing will be integral to any Catholic school or parish program, but especially in those that are gifted with a diverse Christian population.

Catholic principles for dealing with fellow Christians

from other churches among our students are quite clear, as enunciated in the *Directory*:

> In Catholic schools and institutions, every effort should be made to respect the faith and conscience of students or teachers who belong to other Churches or ecclesial Communities. In accordance with their own approved statutes, the authorities of these schools and institutions should take care that clergy of other Communities have every facility for giving spiritual and sacramental ministration to their own faithful who attend such schools or institutions. As far as circumstances allow, with the permission of the diocesan Bishop these facilities can be offered on the Catholic premises, including the church or chapel.[49]

Needless to say, how these policies will be implemented will depend on the demography, school resources and priorities, and diocesan direction.

Opportunities for non-Catholic pastors and priests to minister to their students, as Catholic priests do to theirs, is important. Neighborhood Catholic schools are in a unique position to bring local clergy in their communities into dialogue, about education, church collaboration, service to the families, the rights of the child, and even the dialogue of faith. The dialogue of love is the basis for the dialogue of truth. In this the Catholic educator can be an instrument of ecumenical formation for both school and parish.

When the Holy Father says that the results of the dialogues are to become a "common heritage" he is laying a challenge before the catechist, to provide the bridges of religious reconciliation that are adapted to the learning styles and the curricula appropriate to the particular school or parish. Christians from different churches in the same classroom provide a marvelous learning opportunity for all concerned. This dialogue goes on without any compromise with the truth claims of the Catholic Church about its own fidelity to the tradition. None of the dialogues take away from Catholic understanding of the faith, but they should deepen the understanding of both partners in the dialogue.

Priests and ministers from other communities who have appropriated the Catholic educational vision will be particularly helpful partners in enabling us to discern catechetical priorities and ecumenical agendas in these communities. In generations to come, those schooled in the Gospel of Jesus Christ together in a knowledge of one another's churches and a zeal for unity of Christians, will provide a cadre of leadership that can contribute to the renewal and understanding of our churches and their communion.

The experience of some of our United States schools is interesting, but obviously does not recommend itself elsewhere: The De La Salle Christian Brothers have a San Miguel middle school in Chicago, with only three Catholics, where they use one of the Black Protestant pastors among those who teach religion. Of course, what is important for the Catholic Church, in that context is a) that the school creates a new image and understanding for Catholicism in a community where Catholics are a minority, and b) it is a school that does not rely on Catholic sources alone for funding, though it is explicitly religious and Catholic.

Christian Brothers High School in Memphis has always had a high proportion of other Christian and even Jewish students. Since 1940 these students attended special "ethics" classes. Today the teachers of these classes include a Greek Orthodox graduate of the school, and a Presbyterian deeply involved in the spirituality of St. John Baptist de La Salle, the patron of all teachers. A few years ago, the local Anglican Bishop, who had graduated in 1947, received a distinguished alumnus award. More will be said about the "ethics" curriculum in the Secondary Chapter below (VIII).

There are significant numbers of Eastern Orthodox as well as Eastern Catholics in the U.S., and care needs to be taken to recognize the special relationship and delicate history with the Roman Catholic Church. Marriage preparation of Orthodox and Catholic couples and Orthodox students in Catholic schools are particularly important, since the Orthodox tend to have more stringent requirements than do Catholics for the wedding, but different approaches to a marriage that has dissolved. Also, Catholics are more open to sacramental sharing with the Eastern Orthodox churches than most of the Orthodox communities are with any other churches.

Monsignor Hawker discusses the debate about whether a religion class in which non-Catholics participate should be considered an objective "religious studies" or whether it should be designed to serve the evangelization and catechetical mission of the Church. Certainly, for Christian students who take Catholic religion classes, it can clearly "be viewed as a catechetical experience."[50] However, such classes should be informed by the distinctions and common faith we have ascertained in our ecumenical dialogues, so that all Christians deepen their faith in Christ, their commitment to the unity of Christians, and respect the differences that remain to be resolved between the divided churches. For example, a convinced Methodist in a Catholic school should be invited into a more intimate unity with Christ, our common faith, our differences, a commitment to Catholic – Methodist unity without compromise, and to understand their own Methodist convictions in ecumenical, and faithful ways.

I remember a Presbyterian minister friend who was a graduate of Father Ryan High School in Nashville. He not only attributed his vocation to the priest who taught him religion, he also became an avid reader of the second Vatican Council and a leader in Catholic-Presbyterian dialogue when he became General Presbyter (equivalent of bishop) for the Memphis Presbytery. His understanding of Catholic sacramental theology enabled him to dispel many of the stereotypes of his Protestant colleagues, and to interpret the Catholic liturgical renewal of the 1960s to Catholics and Presbyterians alike. Catholic schools can prepare all Christians for their calling to build the bridges to that unity Christ wills for the Church.

Schools in the African American community, as noted above, provide a unique and important context for Catholic witness and ecumenism. Spirituality and social justice will characterize African-American ecumenism, at this point, more than theological or sacramental questions. When there are young people from these churches or whose parents go to these churches, it will be important to have the opportunity to know the African-American minister and for him to feel welcome in the Catholic community. It will be particularly important for catechesis in Anglo communities to provide Black Protestant worship and dialogue experiences.[51]

In neighborhoods where Catholic schools are committed to serving the poor, these schools will enliven faith in Christ by touching hearts and promoting religious and human education. Catholic educators take the Christian faith of the poor, Catholic, Protestant or Orthodox, with the utmost seriousness. We cannot love the poor without loving and desiring to know the faith and churches of the poor. In the Hispanic/Latino community, Catholic dialogues with Pentecostals will often be an invaluable resource. In other cultures, different dialogue resources will help Catholic educators approach our non-Catholic faculty and students.

However, as educators identifying with the needs of the poor, Catholic educators know that focus on Christ, on the relations in the community, and on the contribution of education to the liberation from the bonds of poverty,

ignorance, and religious and racial prejudice, are basic
in school age students, their teachers and clergy. Such
liberating concerns are necessarily prior to issues about
the nature and unity of the churches in African American
ecumenism. Catholic educators build the human relations
among peoples, churches and schools in the community, best
adapted to human promotion and liberation.

The Catholic school will be the privileged place for
Catholic, Orthodox and Protestant fellow Christians to
work shoulder to shoulder in building the Kingdom through
the common educational enterprise. As Pope John Paul
II says, collaboration will be the school for ecumenism. In
this, the Catholic school will be able to build reconciling
bridges, to which the Catholic Church is committed. These
schools are centers of reconciliation where neither bishops
nor the theologians have the expertise or presence to take
leadership.

Therefore, an integral part of the formation of Catholic
educators will be knowledge of their students, their churches
and their ministers.

Parents

In most cases, both the school and the parents will want
fellow Christians to take Catholic religion classes as is
appropriate. However, the religion faculty in these situations
should be particularly attentive to the dialogues with the
Christian churches to which their students belong. The
teacher will want to be sure that both Catholics and other
students know where we have come in the dialogues, what
the continuing differences are, and what steps are being
taken to resolve these church dividing issues.

It is important that we know the Vatican dialogues with
the particular churches that predominate in the student body.
The ideal would be catechists skilled in the Catholic heritage,
but knowledgeable about other churches represented in
the school and committed to following the ecumenical
developments of our churches together. However, providing
resources for such programs is a challenge.[52]

Monsignor Hawker identifies three levels on which
parents must be engaged before committing themselves
to sending their child to the Catholic school: the Gospel
message as understood by the Catholic Church; the
recognition and appreciation of Christian values; and the
goal of the catechetical enterprise and the Catholic school
environment to assist in a faith response. This recognition
of the catechetical mission of the school does not mean that

the faith response is oriented only to the Catholic Church. If students are convinced Christians, their own Lutheran or Baptist faith, for example, should be strengthened, their differences with Catholicism clarified, and their hopes for unity energized.

The question of tuition for out of parish students in a parish school, Catholic or otherwise, is a delicate point. Again, Monsignor Hawker offers seasoned advice:

> When considering parish schools, it would appear that those who do not support the parish, whether they be Catholic or non-Catholic, should be expected to pay a higher tuition. In my view, then, the determining factor in this instance, is not the religious affiliation or the pupil. Rather it is whether or not the pupil's family is supporting the parish.

> As far as diocesan or private schools are concerned, my opinion is that the rate of tuition should be the same for all of the pupils. I would not expect higher tuitions from non-Catholic students simply because they are non-Catholic.[53]

Where parishes support a school, however, it is appropriate that congregations or families of non-Catholics be given the opportunity to participate in this support. Nevertheless, care must be taken not to use the Catholic school, and its tuition structure, as an unfair incentive for parents to leave their own church to join the parish in order to save money.

As a matter of principle, the Catholic Church does not seek converts among the faithful of other churches. Thus every effort should be made to respect and even promote the participation of students in the life of their own churches, and to avoid practices that could appear to constitute an invitation for a student to join the Catholic Church. As the dialogue with the Oriental Orthodox churches recommends:

> Another practice that can give the impression of seeking converts is the requirement in some places of membership in – and financial contributions to – the Catholic parish where a school is located in order to pay a lower tuition fee. This can appear to be a financial incentive for an Oriental Orthodox family to join the Catholic parish. While the tuition policy of Catholic schools is a complex question and we cannot offer a solution to this problem that would be applicable in all cases, we strongly encourage Catholic pastors to find a way to allow Oriental Orthodox to participate in

their schools without appearing to encourage transfer of membership to the sponsoring Catholic parish. It should be kept in mind that dual church membership is not acceptable for either of our communions.

Sacramental sharing is another area of concern. While the Catholic Church allows the Oriental Orthodox faithful to receive its sacraments in many cases (cf. CIC 844, §3 and CCEO 671), the Oriental Orthodox Churches themselves have varying disciplines on the matter. The Coptic and Ethiopian Orthodox Churches do not allow their faithful to receive sacraments in any church outside the Oriental Orthodox communion, but the Armenian and Syrian Orthodox do allow it in some circumstances. Care should be taken to respect the discipline of the church to which an individual Oriental Orthodox student belongs. At the same time, care should also be taken to prevent an undue sense of exclusion among Oriental Orthodox students. Whenever possible, they should be included as active participants in Liturgies of the Word and other non-sacramental services.

In all these cases, the best solutions can always be reached by direct contact with the local Oriental Orthodox pastors of the students involved. They should be consulted whenever questions arise, and should be invited to participate in the pastoral care of the students who belong to his church by hearing confessions, teaching religious education classes, celebrating liturgical services, etc.[54]

Immigrant and minority groups are particularly susceptible to this sort of subtle proselytism. It may be more effective to finance a school with the help of other churches, whose members go to the Catholic school, just as many parishes may support a centralized school.

Faculty

Teachers in Catholic schools, or at least a core of them, need to be openly committed to the mission of the school and the Gospel, including its ecumenical imperative. Of course, fellow Christians who are not Catholic may be as student oriented, mission directed and committed to the Christian faith as those who identify with our Church. Committed Christian colleagues who are devoted to the ecumenical agenda of their church and open to the developments their church has made with the Catholic Church over the decades are particularly valuable resources. *The Ecumenical Dimension in the Formation of Pastoral Workers* is a resource for faculty and staff development for both Catholic and non-Catholic faculty.[55]

In 1984 Monsignor Hawker outlined expectations that would be part of the interview process for non-Catholic faculty or administrators:

- The applicant should understand and accept the role of the school as a unique pastoral, educational agency of the [Catholic] Church.
- The applicant should understand and be willing to implement the philosophy and goals of the school.
- The applicant should be willing to attend those liturgies and prayer experiences that are celebrated for faculty growth.
- The applicant should be willing to participate in in-service sessions for the faculty intended for spiritual and professional growth.
- The applicant should be willing to attend those liturgies and prayer experiences that are celebrated for the growth of the total school community.
- The applicant should be willing to mirror the Gospel values in relating to the adults and students identified with the school.
- The applicant should understand the importance of integrating the curriculum with the Gospel values espoused by the Church and be willing to do so in his/her subject area.
- The applicant should understand that he/she will not be expected to teach religion especially in those areas that require catechetical witness.[56]

Of course, there will be cases in which particular faculty members from other Christian traditions, appropriately knowledgeable of the subject matter and of the Catholic positions, may be enlisted to collaborate with the religion programming. This may be in schools that have a parallel program of education in religion, values or ethics which is provided as an alternative to the Catholic religion program for the non-Catholic students. It may be in subject areas for which a faculty member may bring a unique expertise which compliments the Catholic members of the religion faculty, like scripture. In these cases, building a strong sense of collegiality in the religion department and a clear sense of accountability to the Catholic mission of the school will be important.

On occasion, non-Catholic parents have been engaged on the catechetical teams of parish religious education programs. In this case, collegiality, continued formation and a sense of common purpose is especially important, since the formation experience of religious education students tends to be less lengthy and intense than that of Catholic school students. On the other hand, the witness of both parents from an interchurch family, intentional and committed to passing on the Christian faith to their Catholic children, is in itself an important witness to the Gospel values on which the catechetical program is centered.

In staff meetings and retreats it will be important to have fellow Christians from other churches share their stories. When agreements are announced between the Catholic Church and particular churches to which significant numbers of the administration, faculty or students belong, recognition of this fact and opportunities for celebration, sharing and common affirmation contribute to the deepening of the experience of faith community in the school.

It is appropriate that the whole faculty be involved in spiritual, religious and catechetical renewal, not just the religion faculty, and not just those who are Catholic. Such programs will also include an ecumenical component, so that fellow Christians will recognize where they are included in Catholic understandings as fellow Christians, the Catholic commitments to dialogue, and Catholic foundations for spiritual ecumenism.

The policy of the Archdiocese of New York, included in the union contract, is an example of this commitment and clarification:

> Effective September 1, 1998, or date of employment, whichever is later, all elementary school teachers must make appropriate progress toward certification in the Catechist Certification Program of the Archdiocese of New York.[57]

This policy is accompanied by a detailed set of specifications, within the contract and a thorough overview of what is expected of all teachers, so that there are no surprises. Those seeking to work in the schools' mission, whatever their religious background, are invited into this rich program of formation as they take on this teaching vocation. It is important for all faculty, and not just the religion faculty, and all teachers, not just the Catholic teachers, to understand the Catholic faith which is at the core of the school's mission.

A religiously diverse faculty can be a great advantage, if there is a strong commitment to the mission of the Catholic school and if, among these teachers, there are those who follow with interest and appreciation the ecumenical commitments of their church with the Catholic Church on the pilgrimage toward unity. There is a caution, however, when there is not diligence in faculty selection, and the question of faith and mission are absent from the selection process, individuals may come on to the faculty without a full commitment to the identity of the Catholic school. This requires both clearly thought out policies on the part of administration and administrative interviews with prospective teachers, and administrators that are informed by the mission and ecumenical vision of the Church and the particular school.

It could be very useful to have committed non-Catholic Christians brought together to listen to their reflections on the Christian mission of our institutions as Christian and Catholic; how their particular heritage has influenced their vocation in our context; and how the Catholic context has enriched their own faith life and church commitment. One can also reflect on the usefulness of religious communities in giving space to lay non-Catholic Christian colleagues to reflect on the relationship of the charism of the founding community to gifts of their own church and its spirituality, if the school is sponsored by a religious order. Indeed, the opportunities for sharing of gifts are limitless.

I n addition to what has already been said about administrators, fellow Christians in our schools and the religion curriculum, those with responsibilities for elementary education will want to be attentive especially to staff preparation, the spirit of dialogue and sacramental preparation.

As noted above, the Archdiocese of New York has a program of formation for all preparing to teach in Catholic elementary schools. Such a program is important for both Catholics and non-Catholics. Even graduates of Catholic universities today may not have had a thorough grounding in the present day formulation of Catholic teaching and Church policies.

Briefing in the ecumenical heritage, policies and priorities of the Catholic Church and the particular diocese will be important components of this orientation. It will be important for even serious Catholic teachers to be able to make distinctions implied in the hierarchy of truths and to have a positive attitude toward other churches and zeal for unity. The distinction between treasured devotional practices and the content of the Catholic faith is particularly important in these early stages of faith formation of all students.

As suggested in the *General Directory for Catechesis,* particular attention will be given to the context in which the school exists, the particular churches in the community and the non-Catholics in the school and faculty, if there are any. As noted above, regular in-service work will be important to keep up with ecumenical and other developments in Catholic life. This will be as important for those whose specialty is a secular subject as for those whose primary commitment is to religious formation.

Direct theological dialogue will not recommend itself to the ordinary elementary classroom situation. There will be opportunities for ecumenical prayer, for meeting leaders of other churches, and possibly for visiting other Christian churches as part of the school program. However, the teachers should have the opportunity to understand the spirit of dialogue, central to Catholic identity, and possibly to participate directly in conversation with other Christians.

Where discussions of doctrine may not be appropriate a spirituality of dialogue can still be communicated. Resources have been provided for parish dialogues, for example, which may be of use to elementary teachers. The United Methodist Catholic dialogue takes up eleven common principles enunciated by Michael Kinnamon.[58] Catholic educator Dr. Margaret Ralph expands on these:

1. **Ecumenical dialogue must have a spiritual orientation. A willingness to be transformed is essential.** (One ramification of this guideline is that people who are positive that they are already the recipients of the whole truth and whose goal is to convert others to their way of thinking are not yet ready for ecumenical dialogue. The union of Churches will involve new insights and mea culpas on everyone's part. We all have something to learn.)

2. **In ecumenical dialogue, participants must be given permission to define themselves, to describe and witness to the faith in their own terms.** (One ramification of this guideline is that those involved in ecumenical dialogue have to learn to listen so that they do not impose on others what they have been told by others to believe. For instance, the fact that a person is not Roman Catholic and does not use the word transubstantiation does not necessarily mean that the person does not believe that Christ is present in the Eucharist.)

3. **In order to be helpful to the group in an interdenominational dialogue, each participant needs to have a clear understanding of his or her own faith and to present it with honesty and sincerity.** (A ramification of this guideline is that our parish adult education programs need to do more than pass on the truths of our faith, the bottom line. We need to offer adult education programs that honor the experience of adults and encourage critical thinking so that they can not only name the truths of our faith, but understand, believe and live out those truths.)

4. **The integrity of each person must be treasured by everyone. As each person speaks, he or she must be mindful not only of his or her own integrity but also of the integrity of the person with whom he or she may be disagreeing. The desired fruit is mutual growth, not victory.** (One ramification of this guideline that I myself took years to learn is that the goal of dialogue is not to persuade our dialogue partners to become Roman Catholic. When others speak we are not to listen with an ear to telling them where their thinking is flawed, but with an ear to appreciating their insights. We all have a great deal to learn.)

5. **Remember that dialogue, particularly at the congregational level, is between people and not just between Churches or ideological positions**. (One ramification of this guideline is that we have to learn to listen with deep respect to each person. Often we think we know what a person thinks when we know that person's denomination. Our presuppositions may not turn out to be accurate.)

6. **Keep the dialogue in the present. Participants do not need to represent or defend their faith communion throughout history.** Present issues are the ones that need to be discussed. (One ramification of this guideline for me is gratitude. I don't want to take responsibility for or defend the crusades or our treatment of Galileo.)

7. **Be willing to separate essentials from nonessentials.** (This guideline once again emphasizes the importance of good adult education. If Catholics do not understand the hierarchy of truths, that is, the relationship of core truths to truths that are derived from those core truths, they will find ecumenical dialogue beyond them.)

8. **Do not insist on more agreement from your partners in dialogue than you would expect from members of your own faith communion.** (I can't but smile when I think about this guideline. In my own diocese, and I think in many dioceses, there is often an alarming division among Roman Catholics. For instance, our Roman Catholic Church teaches us to be contextualists, not fundamentalists, when reading Scripture. When I teach the contextualist approach to Scripture to Catholic adults I often run in to severe criticism… If the level of agreement among Catholics is our bar for an acceptable degree of unity with other

Christians, then we must be closer to our goal than we realize.)

9. **Interpret the faith of your dialogue partner in its best light, rather than in its worst.** (I think we can all understand the importance of this guideline. For example, I would describe myself as completely pro-life. However, I am embarrassed by some of the strategies that some of my fellow pro-life Catholics employ, and I certainly don't want to be associated with a person who would blow up an abortion clinic. Every religious group has its fanatics, and it is not right to judge a group by its least admirable representatives.)

10. **Do not avoid hard issues.** You undoubtedly will not want to tackle these issues first; but once trust has been established, it is important to discuss even difficult issues. (For me inter-communion is such an issue. I am very hesitant to tell others that I do not recognize the ordination of their ministers and this makes their Eucharist questionable in my eyes. However, in discussing this issue I learned more about my own beliefs as well as about how our teaching appears to others.)

11. **Search for ways to turn the increased understanding achieved through dialogue into activities for renewal.** An immediate way to accomplish that is to have it lead to prayer. But as time goes on, other actions will occur to the group. (Shared ecumenical outreach activities are an excellent way to promote ecumenical understanding. Small faith sharing groups are another.)[59]

Dr. Ralph's observations reinforce the importance of adult formation, especially for Catholic school faculty and staff.

Finally, sacramental preparation is an area in which ecumenical sensitivity is important, both for Catholic catechesis and for classes in which other Christians participate. This will also include sensitivities in the formation of parents, Catholic and non-Catholic as well. Parents who are non-Catholic and who are in interchurch families will need to understand the Catholic position on sacramental sharing, what the policy of the diocese is, and what might or might not be possible in the particular situation of the school or parish where the sacraments will be received.

It is important for parents of elementary age students to know these differences and policies before enrolling their children in the Catholic schools so that misunderstandings and hurt feelings can be avoided.

Young people at the age of first sacraments cannot

usually understand the subtleties of Eucharistic doctrine or the ecclesiology which differentiate the churches' theology and practice. However, they can all understand that we are not yet united with fellow Christians; Orthodox, Anglican and Protestant around the common table. We all hunger for communion at the Lord's Table. We respect the saving presence of Christ in other communities and their worship, though we do not take communion in their services.

During the course of a young person's formation, it would be ideal to have experiences of Orthodox and Protestant worship and have an opportunity to reflect both appreciatively on the differences in worship, the common faith that we share in our approach to God, and the steps that are being taken to reconcile our divided churches.

It is particularly important for care to be given to those students who are drawn more deeply into the mystery of the Eucharist by their experience in the Catholic classroom to understand their own tradition, its faith and liturgical practice. On occasion, the Catholic teacher will have to take the initiative to link up a non-Catholic student with an educator or minister of their own tradition so they can understand the sacramental faith that is their own heritage. At all costs, young people should be helped to discriminate between peer pressure and a genuine desire to share the sacraments or an authentic decision to join the Catholic Church.

At the secondary level, where learning becomes more specialized, it is important to have the total faculty community informed about the Church's teaching and its ecumenical priorities, even those faculty members who do not teach religion directly. Campus ministry programs have a wider range of possibilities in programming ecumenical worship, dialogue and social service experiences.

Recruiting the religion faculty is a particular responsibility at this level. In providing for a quality program, it is as important to find teachers with a strong theological training as it is to have science or language teachers who are competent in their fields.

In secondary school more direct attention can be given to the particular churches with which Catholics are in dialogue, to ecumenical social service programs, and to the results of the dialogues.

For many Catholics, their first experience of ecumenism has been through common service in the community, a CROP walk for hunger, pro-life witness, work for civil rights and a host of other civic projects. Often the doctrinal dimension of common baptism or the goal of full sacramental communion comes only after having served with other Christians whose commitment and holiness become clear and whose devotion to Christ is no less central in their lives than that of Catholics.

High schools will want to provide experiences for students in common witness and service. Working on common, ecumenical projects in the community is an important component of formation for Christian service. Providing opportunities for some in confirmation preparation to do service programs in an ecumenical setting, with a minister or congregation of another church, or with a neighborhood or city wide ecumenical agency can help a whole class reflect on the uniqueness and importance of ecumenical approaches to community service.

The Catholic Campaign for Human Development sponsors projects for social change among the poor. Almost all of the projects funded in local communities are ecumenical, some even interfaith including Jewish or Muslim groups. High school students can learn how Christians collaborate by working with one such project in the diocese.

When teaching about the missionary dimension of the Gospel and the social justice witness of the Church in the community, ministers and those working in ecumenical agencies can provide helpful speakers and members of panels, demonstrating how to integrate the ecumenical dimensions of witness into parish life. In some neighborhoods various Christian congregations reach out, together, to newcomers, the unchurched and the alienated, encouraging the unaffiliated to join the Christian church closest to their own traditional roots or affinities. These also provide opportunities for ecumenical service projects.

For some young people, adolescence is a time of testing and ambivalence about the Church and even about the faith. Even while young people are facing serious doubts, service in the community and close collaboration with youth ministers and more committed Christians are important supports during this period of testing. An ecumenical youth group, retreat or service project can be important in providing a place for seeing faith in action, when a person may be in rebellion against the institution, language and even family expression of faith. Young peoples' discussion of their struggles with their various churches can give the developing Catholic a more objective reflection on the Church and the difficulties he or she may be having with it. Such encounters should be discussed in such a way to deepen Christian commitment and to clarify the specifically Catholic character of Christian identity.

The results of the dialogues are vast and continually developing. It is impossible to teach Church History, the sacraments, the church, Christian morals or even the bible without having some knowledge of the rich resources of the dialogues. Teachers' guides would provide a great assistance to high school teachers in particular if these agreements and clarifications were made available according to the subjects being taught. Summaries of some of the dialogues do exist.[60] However, for high school students, special projects, church visits and papers and searches on the web can all contribute to an interest in the unity of Christians and understanding of Catholic approaches to unity.[61]

Catholics are not fundamentalists. We share a great love for a liturgical and critical approach to reading the bible, going deeper than a narrow literalistic interpretation. It is important that young people at this age learn a love for the bible and begin to integrate it into their devotional and intellectual life. Just as they learn the scientific method as one way of appreciating nature, they can come to learn critical biblical scholarship as a way of seeing more deeply into the truth of God's revelation. Intellectual excitement about the Christian faith and its methods of exploration can touch both the mind and heart in such a way that young people in these formative years can be drawn into a process of life long learning. Some of them can be motivated to see themselves drawn to a vocation of biblical or theological scholarship in service to truth in the Church. The sacred Scriptures are one of the most important bonds between Catholics and fellow Christians.

A zeal for history of the Church, its spiritual and sacramental life will help adolescents appreciate the lights and shadows of Christian history. It will help them to embark themselves on the journey of a pilgrim people actively responsive to God's call in human history as their forbearers have been. They are at an age to begin to understand the Church's teaching on the development of doctrine, the hopes for ecumenical reconciliation and the service that scientific Christian history can provide to the pastoral life of the Church.

As was noted above, some high schools with a large population of non-Catholics may wish to provide a parallel program for those non-Catholic students who wish an alternative to the Catholic religion classes. The example of the "ethics" classes provided in Christian Brothers High School in Memphis, Tennessee is an illustration. It shows some classes that occur in both syllabi, and some that are special to each.

For example, the Hebrew Scriptures (Old Testament) and community service occur in both programs, though for the religion syllabus, the latter is coupled with Catholic social teaching. For other years, the ethics curriculum consists in a year of psychology, a year of comparative religion, and a multicultural approach to morality. The morality course closely parallels what is found in a Catholic religion course on personal morality and Catholic social teaching, covering many of the same issues but from a wider ethical basis. Depending on the composition of a particular school, courses in Jewish-Christian relations, the history of Christianity, interreligious dialogue, or Christian Scriptures could be designed to serve both Catholic catechetical priorities and the intellectual faith development of believers who were not Catholic.

As the Church moves more deeply into communion with other Christians and our programs of catechesis attempt to keep pace, our secondary curricula and school context will be an important locus for leadership training. It is during the adolescent years that the intellectual imagination, and often the career horizons of young Christians, begin to take shape. Fascination about and love for the Church is a central goal of the spiritual formation in this period of development. Active engagement in the ecumenical mission of the Church, like social justice, liturgical awareness, and biblical enthusiasm are important resources for the secondary school teacher in bringing alive the religious imagination of the adolescent.

IX

Catholic Higher Education

The role of Catholic colleges and universities is explicitly outlined in the ecumenical *Directory*. These characteristics are to be found widely in U.S. college and university institutions:

[Universities] are called on to give sound ecumenical formation. Examples of the appropriate measures they may take are these:

a. to foster, when the subject calls for it, an ecumenical dimension to methods of teaching and research;

b. to organize discussions and study days on ecumenical questions;

c. to organize conferences and meetings for joint study, work and social activity, setting aside time for enquiry into Christian principles of social action and the means of putting them into practice. These occasions, whether involving only Catholics or bringing together Catholics and other Christians, should promote cooperation as far as possible with other advanced institutes in the area;

d. space could be given in university journals and reviews to reports on ecumenical events, and also to deeper ecumenical studies, with preference given to comments on the documents resulting from inter-Church dialogue;

e. in academic halls of residence there is very much to recommend good relations between Catholics and other Christian students. With suitable guidance, they can learn, through these relations, to live together in a deeper ecumenical spirit and be faithful witnesses of their Christian faith;

f. it is important to give emphasis to prayer for unity, not only during the Week of Prayer for this purpose but also at other times during the year. Depending on circumstances of place and persons, and in conformity with the existing rules about shared worship, joint retreats under the guidance of a spiritual master, may also be envisaged;

g. there is a wide field of common witness in social or welfare works. Students should be trained and encouraged in this-not only theology students, but also those of other faculties, such as law, sociology and political science. By their contribution these students will help to promote and realize such initiatives;

h. chaplains, student counselors and professors will have a particular concern to carry out their tasks in an ecumenical spirit, especially by organizing some of the initiatives indicated above. This obligation demands from them a deep knowledge of the doctrine of the Church, an adequate competence in academic subjects, unfailing prudence and a balanced attitude: all these qualities should enable them to help their students to harmonize their own life of faith with openness to others.[62]

Our boards and administrative teams in Catholic higher education vary widely in the diversity of their composition, experience and communities served. The ways we do selection and formation are adapted to the needs of our institutions, and hopefully also to the vision of the Church. The ecumenical dimension of that mission can only be one element of the vision, formation and task of leadership tailored to each institutions' needs and context. However, there is always a danger for it to be either taken for granted, or dismissed as insignificant.

Boards, like students and faculties, are often religiously pluralistic. It can be helpful to provide both interreligious and ecumenical partners on our boards, opportunities to lead in prayer and to understand developing Catholic relations with their particular communities. On occasion one can give a copy of a new dialogue result, say between Orthodox and Catholics, to an Orthodox colleague.

It is important to understand the contribution of curriculum and campus ministry to the relationship with the particular communities to which board, student and faculty belong. If a particular faculty member or administrator has demonstrated their contribution to unity, mutual understanding and common witness, an opportunity can be found to celebrate or witness with the board or administration.

As *Ex Corde Ecclesiae* notes, universities provide an opportunity for research and service in the community that fosters unity among Christians. Training of catechists is a particular calling of Catholic institutions of higher education. These training programs will have an ecumenical component, and often will serve other Christian catechists in churches beyond the Catholic community. This common learning of catechists together is both a resource for their own dialogue and enrichment for their teaching. Theologians who serve on the ecumenical dialogues are a resource on campus and in the wider community.

University administrators can help Catholic board members see the inherent commitment to Christian unity and interreligious outreach as central to the Catholic identity of the institution, support of the Magisterium, and the economic and recruiting well being of the institution. For example, the oldest Jesuit university in the United States, Georgetown in the nation's capital, has taken on a full time assistant to the president to promote interreligious concerns in the program and policy of the university.

X

Conclusion

The Catholic school and parish catechetical program are only two venues for the nurturing of Christians' commitment to the unity of the Church, albeit privileged ones. Schools and parishes do well to take account, and on occasion provide, adult Christian education programs that enrich the faith of the parents and wider community. This can include an understanding of other churches, Catholic ecumenical principles, the results of our dialogue, and work together as churches.

Should not students come away from their catechetical formation and Catholic schooling with an impatience for the unity of the Church and with skills and knowledge to equip them for deepening the bonds of our parishes, dioceses and churches as they seek to realize God's will? Should they not be preparing to live, work and pray with fellow Christians with whom they already share more than divides them?

Pope John Paul II continually reminds us that we share more, with fellow Christians, than divides us. In speaking of the ordination of women in the Anglican Communion he was most clear, with Episcopal and Catholic bishops, that we should not be surprised nor deterred from the goal of full communion by new challenges we face, like differences over the ordination of women.[63]

If we can light a fire among our young people that lets them love the Church and its sacraments and seeks to deepen our common life with other fellow Christians, have we not made a great contribution, as Catholic educators, to what the Spirit is doing in the world?

Catholic educators have a unique role, not only in supporting the vocation to unity of the school, parish, diocese and universal Church. They help their students and staff colleagues come to conversion, participate in the pilgrimage, and learn the rich results of our encounters with other Christians.

Unity is an affirmation all Catholic Christians make, but the experiences, the knowledge and the action in the community implicit in this affirmation can only come about by diligent educational pursuit.

As Pope John Paul II affirms for all of us: "Concern for restoring unity pertains to the whole church, faithful and clergy alike. It extends to everyone, according to the ability of each, whether it be exercised in daily Christian living or in theological and historical studies."(UUS 19) The Catholic educator has a significant contribution to make to this pilgrimage which is the calling of the whole people of God.

The parish is a primary locus for Christian nurture and ecumenical activity. Even when the school is not parish based, it prepares Christians for a life that will find its mature focus in parish community. Knowing the particular churches in the vicinity of students' parishes and the relationships that are in place or need to be nourished gives concrete content to the school and parish catechetical faith community experience and curricular content.

1. *General Directory for Catechesis,* Washington: United States Catholic Conference, 1998, 78-79. (GDC) http://www.vatican.va/roman_curia/ congregations/cclergy/documents/rc_con_ccatheduc_doc_17041998_ directory-for-catechesis_en.html

2. John Paul, *Ut Unum Sint:* On Commitment to Ecumenism, *Origins,* 25: 4, June 8, 1995, 49 - 72. http://www.vatican.va/holy_father/john_paul_ii/ encyclicals/documents/hf_jp-ii_enc_25051995_ut-unum-sint_en.html, #19, 20.(UUS)

3. Directory for the Application of Principles and Norms on Ecumenism, *Origins,* Vol. 23: No. 9., # 68. http://www.vatican.va/roman_curia/pontifical_councils/chrstuni/ documents/rc_pc_chrstuni_doc_25031993_principles-and-norms-on-ec umenism_en.html (Directory)

4. *Directory,* 20.

5. Dean Hoge, et. al., *Young Adult Catholics: Religion in the Culture of Choice,* Notre Dame: University of Notre Dame Press, 2002, 6.

6. To be Catholic or Not to Be: Is It Still the Question? Catholic Identity and Religious Education Today. *Horizons,* 25 (2), p.179.

7. Hoge, 17.

8. Ibid. 16.

9. *Decree on Ecumenism*, http://www.vatican.va/archive/hist_councils/ ii_vatican_council/documents/vat-ii_decree_19641121_unitatis- redintegratio_en.html

10. GDC.

11. Ibid.

12. James Hawker, Thea Bowman, *The Non-Catholic in the Catholic School,* Washington: National Catholic Education Association, 1984, Bowman, p. 21.

13. GCD # 86 b. See # 133 for discussion of inculturation of catechetical material in local contexts, and # 158 for the significance of the local community as resource and point of reference.

14. Hawker, p. 4.

15. Pontifical Council for Promoting Christian Unity, "The Ecumenical Dimension in the Formation of Pastoral Workers," *Origins*, 27:39, March 19, 1998, 653-661.(EF) http://www.vatican.va/roman_curia/pontifical_councils/chrstuni/ documents/rc_pc_chrstuni_doc_16031998_ecumenical-dimension_ en.html

16. *Directory*, #9.

17. *Directory*, # 30-34.

18. UUS, # 41, 72, 80.

19. http://www.vatican.va/roman_curia/pontifical_councils/chrstuni/sub- index/index_weeks-prayer.htm

20. http://www.geii.org/#wpcu

21. UUS, #16.

22. *Directory*, 23.

23. Hawker, p. 5.

24. *Ecumenical Formation*, # 22-26.

25. Hawker, p. 4.

26. *Policy Manual for Administrators,* 1998, # 621.

27. See note 5.

28. Hawker, p. 7.

29. Proselytism is distinguished from evangelization, as an unfair or coercive pressure placed on an individual to change his or her faith or community. Cf. "Evangelization, Proselytism and Common Witness," http://www.prounione.urbe.it/dia-int/pe-rc/doc/e_pe-rc_pent04.html

30. *Directory*, # 99.

31. Phan, p.171

32. *Directory*, # 55-56.

33. Ibid., # 129.

34. Ibid., 130-131.

35. I.e. For example, *Ecumenical Handbook for the Roman Catholic Dioceses of Kentucky* http://www.ccky.org/PDF%20Files/1995%20Ec umenical%20Handbook%20update%2012-2003.pdf *Pastoral Manual, Diocese of Rockville Centre on Long Island*   Section I, Chapter xiii - Ecumenical Issues. pages 215a-k and 216-220. *Statements by the Catholic Bishops of Pennsylvania, Questions and Answers on the Eucharist* # 17. http://www.pacatholic.org/ bishops'%20statements/eucharist.htm

36. Peter Casarella, Raúl Gómez, *El Cuerpo de Cristo: The Hispanic Presence in the U.S. Catholic,* New York: Crossroads Publishing, 1998.

37. *Directory*, # 74.

38. UUS, # 80.

39. Ibid., #6.

40. Lukas Vischer and Harding Meyer eds., Growth in Agreement Reports and Agreed Statements of Ecumenical Conversations on a World Level , New York: Paulist Press, 1984. William Rusch, Harding Meyer, Jeffrey Gros, eds., Growth in Agreement II, Geneva/Grand Rapids: World Council of Churches/Wm B Eerdmans, 2000. http: //www.prounione.urbe.it/dia-int/e_dialogues.html

41. Ann Riggs, Eamon McManus, Jeffrey Gros, *Introduction to Ecumenism,* New York: Paulist Press, 1998. Fredrick Bliss, *Catholic and Ecumenical: History and Hope,* Ashland: Sheed and Ward, 1999. Gideon Goosen, *Bringing Churches Together: A Popular Introduction to Ecumenism,* Geneva: World Council of Churches, 2001. Allan Laubenthal, *Catholic Teaching on Ecumenism,* Westlake, OH: Center for Learning, 2003.

42. Ronald G. Roberson, *The Eastern Christian Churches,* Washington: U.S. Catholic Conference, 1995. http://www.cnewa.org/ ecc-introduction.htm
These Catholic churches are: Byzantine (Melkite, Ukrainian, Ruthenian, Romanian, Bulgarian, Hungarian, Slovak), Armenian, Coptic, Ethiopian, Syriac, Syro-Malankara, Syro-Malabar, Chaldean, Maronite and a few smaller groups. All but the Maronite have counterparts that are Orthodox.

43. Jeffrey Gros, *That All May Be One: Ecumenism,* Chicago: Loyola University Press, 2000.

44. *Journey to the Fullness of Life: A Report on the Implementation of the Rite of Christian Initiation of Adults in the United States,* Washington, D.C.: United States Catholic Conference, 2000. http://www.usccb.org/ evangelization/journey.htm

45. Ronald A. Oakham, *One at the Table: The Reception of Baptized Christians,* Chicago: Liturgical Training Publications, 1995.

46. Center for Marriage and Family, Ministry to Interchurch Marriages, Omaha: Creighton University, 1999. *A Guide on Catholic-Orthodox Marriages,* Washington: U.S. Catholic Conference, 1998. Michael Lawler, *Ecumenical Marriage and Remarriage: Gift and Challenge to the Church,* Mystic: Twenty Third Publications, 1990. Ronald G. Roberson, ed., *Oriental Orthodox-Roman Catholic Pastoral Relationships and Interchurch Marriages,* Washington, U.S. Catholic Conference, 1995. Bishop Patrick Cooney & Rev. John Bush, *Interchurch Families: Resources for Ecumenical Hope,* Washington: U.S. Conference of Catholic Bishops, 2002. George Kilcourse, *Double Belonging: Interchurch Families and Christian Unity,* New York: Paulist 1992.

47. Hawker, p. 1.

48. Ibid 10.

49. *Directory*, #141.

50. Hawker, p. 11.
51. William Watley, *Singing the Lord's Song in a Strange Land,* Geneva: World Council of Churches, 1992.
52. Cf. Ann Riggs, Eamon McManus, Jeffrey Gros, *Introduction to Ecumenism,* New York: Paulist Press, 1998.
53. Ibid 15
54. *Oriental Orthodox Catholic Dialogue, Guidelines Concerning The Pastoral Care of Oriental Orthodox Students in Catholic Schools,* 1999. http://www.usccb.org/seia/oriental.htm
55. Cf. note 15.
56. Hawker, p. 7.
57. Policy of the Archdiocese of New York, Article XXX, a.
58. United Methodist Catholic Dialogue, *Yearning for Unity: Small Group Parish Study Resources,* Washington: U.S. Catholic Conference, 2000, p.27.
59. "Ecumenical Implications for Catholic Evangelization," in *Catholic Evangelization in an Ecumenical and Interreligious Society,* Washington: United States Conference of Catholic Bishops, 2004.
60. *Thirty Years of Mission and Witness: United Methodist Roman Catholic Dialogue,* Washington/Nashville: United States Catholic Conference/ United Methodist Commission on Christian Unity and Interreligious Concerns, 2001. *The Lutheran-Catholic Quest for Visible Unity: Harvesting Thirty Years of Dialogue,* Chicago/Washington: Evangelical Lutheran Church in America/United States Catholic Conference, 1998. *Journey in Faith: Forty Years of Reformed-Catholic Dialogue,* Washington: U.S. Conference of Catholic Bishops, 2004.
61. http://www.usccb.org/seia/index.htm
    http://www.prounione.urbe.it/dia-int/e_dialogues.html
    http://www.wcc-coe.org/wcc/english.html
    http://www.ncccusa.org/about/unityhome.html
62. *Directory,* #89
63. In "One in Mind and Heart: a Pilgrimage of Anglican and Roman Catholic Bishops," *One in Christ,* 31:2, 1995, 171-184.